# Listen to The Music

## The Words You Don't Hear
## When You Listen To The Music

## Timeless Lessons of Life

*As seen through the lyrics of the singers and
songwriters of the 60's & 70's*

**Compiled and Written by**
Steve Richards

authorHOUSE®

*AuthorHouse™*
*1663 Liberty Drive*
*Bloomington, IN 47403*
*www.authorhouse.com*
*Phone: 1-800-839-8640*

*First published by AuthorHouse 9/18/2009*

*ISBN: 978-1-4490-0880-2 (e)*
*ISBN: 978-1-4490-0879-6 (sc)*

*Printed in the United States of America*
*Bloomington, Indiana*

*This book is printed on acid-free paper.*

*Cover Photo Credits*
*Concert photo © Wolfgang Rattay/Reuters/Corbis*
*All other photos © PRPhotos*

# Online Access and Password

Thanks for purchasing <u>Listen To The Music</u>! You've been listening to the music for years but have you ever really heard the words? This book highlights the lyrics from a wide range of 60's & 70's artists and their songs. With over 250 lyric excerpts, you are sure to find a number from your favorite songs... some you know by heart and others you may have forgotten.

Many of the lyrics are thought provoking, some are whimsical and humorous, others carry a serious message, and many inspire or motivate. Because of limitations on the book's size, only 25% of the lyrics in the library have been included in the book. Many other equally thought provoking lyrics can be found on the book's website – over 1100 in all, taken from 750 songs performed by over 160 artists. Purchasing the book gives you access to the entire library!

**How do I find the website?**
Go to: www.listentothemusiclyrics.com

**Do I need a user ID to enter the website?**
Yes. The user ID you must use is **ClassicRock**

**Will I need a password to access all of the songs and lyrics?**
Yes. Your password is – **6070music**

**What will I find when I get into the website?**
The website offers a number of cool features...
1. Access to 1100 excerpts from the lyrics of over 750 classic rock songs
2. Search the library by artist
3. Search the library by song title
4. With one simple click, purchase and download any of the over 750 songs on Amazon.com

**I have a favorite song with some great lyrics. How do I get it included?**

Great question! While every effort has been made to be as inclusive and comprehensive as possible, I know that there are many other great songs from the 60's & 70's that didn't make the first cut. If you have lyrics from a favorite song, please email me the song title and the specific excerpt and I will add it to the library. My email address is: **steve@listentothemusiclyrics.com.**

Again, thanks for purchasing the book. I hope you enjoy reading it as much as I enjoyed writing it. If you like it, please recommend it to a friend.

*Steve*

# Acknowledgements

My sincere thanks to Brad DiBaggio and Sherie Johnson from DiBaggio Designs of San Antonio, Texas (*DiBagioDesign.com*). Their creativity, persistence and patience resulted in visually striking design elements that compliment the book's style. Brad's enthusiasm and diligence in developing the *ListenToTheMusicLyrics.com* website reflects his passion for music as a musician and song writer. Together, their insights and suggestions along with their ability to visually present my vision for the book created energy and excitement at a critical time in the development of the project.

My family was instrumental in the writing of this book. My wife Susann was my editor in chief gently pointing out areas that "need more work" and providing encouragement throughout the process. Our daughter Cristy helped me organize and manage my research and the over 1100 lyric quotes while our son Glen provided creative advice and direction that ultimately led to the final cover design.

# Dedication

Each of us lives our everyday life in our own way. Some will be seen as having been more or less successful than others, some will have more money, bigger homes, and more expensive cars. Many will work into their 70's out of necessity while others will retire financially secure in their 50's. Some will know the joy of raising a family while others are content to live life alone.

As we reach the latter stages of our lives when professional success and personal achievement are less important, the size of fortunes amassed, the value of a home or the power and status achieved means little. In the end, we will all be judged by the same simple criteria... the families we have raised and the lives we have touched along life's journey. Children learn fundamental values such as honesty, integrity, compassion, love, and selflessness from their parents who demonstrate those values through their everyday actions and deeds. Children pass those values on to their children and that's our life's true legacy.

What we have done to impact the lives of others is another measure of our true success in life. Leading a non-profit organization, volunteering at a homeless shelter, or working with special needs children are but a few of the endless opportunities to serve others. In selflessly serving others, we seldom see the results of our efforts, but in the end, lives are touched in ways that we do not fully understand.

It may come as no surprise that this book is dedicated to my family. To Susann, my wife of 41 years who, while pursuing her teaching career, moved our home and family 12 times in 27 years always with a sense of excitement and optimism for the next new adventure that lay ahead. To our daughter and son, Cristy and Glen, who have always made us exceedingly proud, not for what they have achieved but because of the kind of people they have become. And to Frank and Vanessa, our "other" son and daughter, who decided to share their lives with Cristy and Glen and, in so doing, have given us the immense joy of grandchildren.

As the Eagles song goes.... "Life's been good to me!"

# Contents

## Introduction

## Putting It In Perspective

## The Words You Don't Hear
## When You Listen to The Music

# Epilogue

# Appendix

# Resources

# Index

Music makes you happy

~

Music makes you sad

~

Music grounds you and gives you roots

~

Music inspires

~

Music takes you to another place and
time...
even if for just a brief moment

~

Music pulls lost memories deep from within
your soul

# The Rolling Stones

To view the entire photo album go to
**listentothemusiclyrics.com**

# Introduction

"A long, long time ago
I can still remember
How that music used to make me smile
Do you believe in rock n' roll
Can music save your mortal soul?"
*(Don McLean ~ American Pie)*

The music of the 60's and 70's reflects the turbulent events of two decades marked by unprecedented social, political, and economic change. The complex challenges Americans faced in the 60's and 70's are strikingly similar to the times we find ourselves in today. Unlike then, today's pop artists do not speak to the significant issues shaping the world around us, including an unpopular two-front war, an economy in crisis, climate change and divisive social issues. Attracting tabloid and media attention by what an artist is (or is not) wearing or with whom they are seen seems more important to the artist than their music. The MySpace, Twitter, Facebook, Instant Messaging, iPod (not that I don't have three!) generation is looking for entertainment that is visually stimulating and immediately accessible. With You-Tube and streaming videos to your laptop or iPod, Gen-Y'ers and "Millennials" are more entertained by what they see than by what they hear. For those reasons, today's singers and songwriters focus more on style than on substance because that's what sells music and draws young fans to concerts.*

---

*\* The notable exception is Country Music which continues to grow in popularity across all generations. Country Music talks about family, patriotism, love and everyday life in a way that all can relate to.*

1

Most singers and songwriters of the 60's and 70's were born during or just after World War II. As such, they were on the leading edge of the Baby Boomer generation. They were raised by parents born during the Great Depression who, because of their experiences, taught their children to be independent, self-reliant, free thinkers which profoundly influenced their music. These artists vividly expressed through their music what people were experiencing during those turbulent times. Raw emotions of love, anger, fear, frustration and hopes and dreams for a better world were common themes in the lyrics of the music of the 60's & 70's.

The first Baby Boomers graduated from high school in 1964 and from college in 1968. The last Boomers entered high school in 1978 and entered college in 1982. But this book is not written only for the Boomers (although they may find deeper meaning in the lyrics since they grew up during these times) because the music of the 60's and 70's is as popular today as it was 40 years ago. This is clearly evident by the fact that an eclectic mix of teens, Gen Y'ers, Gen X'ers and yes, even grey haired Boomers are attending record-breaking concerts by artists like the Eagles, Rolling Stones, Tina Turner, Elton John, Billy Joel, Rod Stewart, and Jimmy Buffett. The music of the 60's and 70's has cross-generational appeal, standing the test of time like no other music in American history.

Growing up, Boomers danced to the music, studied to the music (or at least tried to), listened to the music at work, and sometimes even made love to the music (say it isn't so!). In the 60's, we were busy living (or should I say exploring) life, skipping class or trying to find a date for the next fraternity party. Blame it on youthful exuberance, a short attention span, or other distractions: while we listened to the music, we seldom heard the words to our favorite songs. Many of us are now at a point in our lives where we have the time, the patience, and, most importantly, the perspective to truly appreciate the wit, wisdom, and touch of philosophy within the lyrics of many of our favorite songs. Indulging in a bit of retrospect on our younger years is OK. But this is not easy for those of us who came of age in the 60's and 70's. After all, we are a Type A generation of work-a-holic planners, doers, and overachievers.

"Some things never seem to last
Ain't it funny how we missed the past"
*(Elton John ~ Where Have All the Good Times Gone)*

I was not sure what I would find when I began this project. Undoubtedly, there would be great music and lots of it. However, I was surprised by the vast number of insightful lyrics that I found, the diversity of the artists' styles, as well as by the messages and the emotions about life and the world around them that were expressed through their lyrics. In the end, I learned more than I ever expected about the music that continues to affect my life. The music of singers and songwriters such as Bob Dylan, Jim Croce, Carole King, Paul Simon, Neil Young, and John Lennon had meaning and purpose often protesting injustice or singing of life's trials and tribulations. Some artists focused on their musical style as much as on their lyrics, experimenting with non-traditional rock instruments such as the organ, mandolin, harmonica, tambourine, electric keyboard, synthesizer, and steel guitar. One of the most successful and popular rock bands of the era was the Doobie Brothers whose distinctive sound was due in part to their having two drummers to accentuate the beat and add depth to their music.

Many Motown artists including The Temptations and James Brown along with mainstream groups like Chicago and

The Eagles incorporated brass into their arrangements to give their music a unique and rich sound. Other artists used concert orchestras to add elegance and sophistication to their arrangements. The Beatles, "Uncle Albert/Admiral Halsey," The Rolling Stones, "You Can't Always Get What You Want," and "Sunset Grille" by The Eagles are great examples of intricate arrangements combined with orchestration. Incorporating the London Bach Boys Choir into the Rolling Stones' "You Can't Always Get What You Want" took rock to a whole new level.

Unforgettable harmony distinguishes groups like the Beach Boys, The Beatles, Crosby, Stills, Nash & Young, The Eagles and The Bee Gees while expressive choreography and perfectly performed dance routines added flair and showmanship to the music of many Soul/Motown artists such as James Brown, the Temptations, The Spinners, and The Jackson 5. Some artists were able to consistently combine great music with meaningful lyrics. Not surprisingly, they remain the most recognized and successful 60's and 70's artists today – The Beatles, The Rolling Stones, Elton John, The Eagles, Rod Stewart, Billy Joel, Styx and Jimmy Buffett are but a few who have enjoyed musical careers spanning three to four decades.

Some songwriters were storytellers painting vivid pictures of their life experiences through their lyrics. Billy Joel wrote about growing up and living in New York City with songs such as "Uptown Girl," "New York State of Mind," "Street Life Surrender," and "Scenes from an Italian Restaurant." Bruce Springsteen wrote about his blue collar roots, growing up in New Jersey and living through the decline of the steel and coal industries in Pennsylvania with songs such as "My Hometown," "Meeting Across the River," "Better Days," "Glory Days," and "Factory." John Denver talks of a simple life high in the Colorado Rocky Mountains while Jimmy Buffett transports us to a far away, secluded Caribbean beach and to a magical bar

4

in a place called "Margaritaville". Other artists wrote songs with messages that spoke directly to certain issues or groups. Few will remember that early in his career, James Brown spoke to young inner-city blacks about staying in school, staying off drugs and being proud to be black with songs such as "Don't Be A Dropout" and "Say It Loud, I'm Black and I'm Proud." Stevie Wonder sang about life in the ghetto in his song "Village Ghetto Land," the need for racial tolerance in "Black Man," and he decries South African apartheid in his song "It's Wrong."

"I hope you can hear
What the words and the music have to say"
(Engelbert Humperdinck ~ After the Lovin')

Much of the music of the 60's and 70's, like the music of today, speaks of love and relationships... looking for love, finding love, loosing love, looking for love all over again, etc. There is poetry in the lyrics of love songs of the 60's and 70's from songwriters like Carole King, Rod Stewart, Neil Diamond, and Fleetwood Mac's Stevie Nicks and Christine McVie – enough to fill an entire book. Emotional songs dealing with despair and loneliness are a close second to songs about love and relationships. Simon and Garfunkel built a musical career around songs of loneliness, despair, and depression. Who can forget the haunting melody of Simon and Garfunkel's the "Sound of Silence." However, the lyrics which include "Hello darkness my old friend..." definitely do not take you to a happy place!

I love Soul/Motown music and can't sit still when The Temptations, Four Tops or The Spinners come on my iPod or Satellite radio. Love and relationships are a common theme in Soul/Motown music as it was in other genres but some Soul/

R&B artists like Barry White, Al Green, and Marvin Gaye took love songs to a whole different level. In the end, Soul/Motown brought a beat and rhythm to music unlike any other evoking a sense of power and freedom that was expressed through the way that people danced to it. Disco? With the notable exception of the Bee Gees, Disco was all thrust and no vector, all style and no substance. You knew that Disco wouldn't last when one of the big hits in the late 70's was a disco version of the "I Love Lucy" TV theme song!

As they matured, some artists' musical style began to evolve as they moved into the 70's and beyond. In particular, Elton John and The Beatles refined their musical style and message with more subtle and sophisticated arrangements and more emotional lyrics. Compare Elton John's "Hercules," "Crocodile Rock" and "Honkey Cat" written in 1972 and 1973 with his late 80's and early 90's albums *Sleeping With The Past*, *The One*, and *Duets*. Listen to The Beatles "Love Me Do" and "I Want to Hold Your Hand" performed in 1963, then listen to "Here Comes the Sun" from 1969 and "The Long and Winding Road" from 1970 and you will see what I mean. A few artists – such as Rod Stewart with his "Great American Songbook" series and Elton John composing music for Tony Award-winning plays such as *The Lion King* and *Aida* – have successfully "reinvented" themselves launching fresh, new musical careers with even broader appeal.

Finally, I discovered groups that had great music but whose lyrics sometimes lacked substance and in certain songs were just plain perplexing. America is one of my favorite light-rock groups and I have all of their songs on my iPod, but if you ever listen carefully to the words to "Tin Man," "Muskrat Love," "Ventura Highway," or "Horse with No Name," you will walk away mumbling to yourself. Someone please explain to me... what are "...alligator lizards in the air" (from "Ventura

Highway")? Something that escaped from the San Diego Zoo and was found wandering down Ventura Highway? And just exactly what is "Muskrat Love"? How about "...and cause never was the reason for the evening or the tropic of Sir Galahad" (from "Tin Man")? Sorry, I'm lost. These guys were either trying too hard to be creative or you've got to wonder what they were doing just before they wrote these lyrics. Queen and Jefferson Airplane both had good music but lyrics that sometimes confused and confounded you. If you need proof, just check out Grace Slick and Jefferson Airplane's "White Rabbit." OK... blame it on Timothy Leary or just growing up and living in San Francisco in the late 60's!

> "Ain't it funny how we all turned out
> I guess we are the people our parents warned us about"
> *(Jimmy Buffett ~ We're The People Our Parents Warned us About)*

This book focuses on the artists who launched their careers in the 60's and 70's and whose music was influenced by the events of the times. Many of these artists enjoyed success well beyond the 70's, and for that reason, I have selectively drawn lyrics from some songs recorded in the 80's and 90's. You will notice a few lyrics from Elvis Presley. Elvis essentially had two separate and distinct careers. The first spanned most of the 1950's and into the early 60's when his popularity faded. Elvis reinvented himself in the late 60's when he launched his extremely successful multi-year engagement at the International Hotel in Las Vegas. The Elvis Presley lyrics found in this book come from songs featured during his later years while performing in Las Vegas.

As you read the lyrics in this book, recognize that they have been taken out of context. Most are straight forward and carry the message that the singer/songwriter intended. However, in a few instances, the lyrics as presented in the book may have a very different meaning than when you read it within the context of the entire song. For example, in Simon and Garfunkel's song "I Am a Rock," the lyrics "I am a rock – I am an island" conveys strength, conviction and self confidence. However, the song talks of a depressed and lonely soul who has neither friends nor love in his life... and who seems to like it that way. The final stanza of the song... "And a rock feels no pain and an island never cries" evokes quite the opposite emotion from the first stanza. Wow... that's heavy, brother.

I have organized these lyric excerpts according to various stages of life... from growing up and finding your soul mate to raising a family and arriving at that stage of your life where you have become wiser, not older. While these lyrics will hopefully bring back memories, they can also be put to practical use. As I describe in the epilogue, the messages contained in many of these lyrics provide the perfect vehicle for you to talk to your children and their children about your life experiences. By bringing these or other of your favorite lyrics to life by telling a story of your experiences or lessons learned the hard way may help guide them through life, now and in the future. At 12 years old while my father was showing me how to saw a piece of lumber, he said... "Always remember the Carpenter's Creed... *"Measure twice and saw once"*. We talked about its meaning in the workshop that afternoon and the quote has stuck with me throughout my life. Being impatient, as many of us are, it surely has kept me from making even more mistakes than I have already made.

Some parents today have abdicated their role in developing strong values and character within their children, looking instead to the schools to fill that role. Schools simply cannot take the place of good parenting and do not have the time to instill fundamental values in their students. That responsibility continues to fall on the family, just as it always has. In today's social networking and instant messaging generation, instilling core values, sound moral principles, and honesty and integrity is needed more than ever before. Those of us who lived through the turbulent times of the 60's and 70's have the unique opportunity and in fact a responsibility to help fill that role within our families.

## "The secret of life is enjoying the passage of time"
### (James Taylor ~ Secret of Life)

This book is about living life. With the benefit of crystal clear 20-20 hindsight, we now realize that we could have avoided some of the mistakes we made in life... "If only I knew then what I know now!" Some lyrics are simply one or two lines while others may be a complete stanza. These brief glimpses into the lyrics of songs that you know by heart may simply take you back to those days of youthful exuberance, innocence, and exploration. However, others may help you recall some of your life experiences that are worth sharing with your family. I have found, as hopefully you will, that many of the lyrics contain timeless lessons of life that are as relevant today as they were yesterday.

I have never played a musical instrument and can't even hum in tune so why did I write a book about the music of the 60's and 70's? The answer is really quite simple... the music that I grew up with has impacted my life. An athletic scholarship took me to The Ohio State University in Columbus, Ohio and during my first semester, I was asked to become a member of the Sigma

Alpha Epsilon fraternity. I remember my first fraternity party when the band played "Soul Man" by Sam & Dave, the music brought out something in me that I never realized I had. While I couldn't sing or play an instrument, I had "the moves" on the dance floor! After four great years at Ohio State guided by a personal philosophy of never letting my education get in the way of my fun, I graduated in 1968 and moved on to what would become a highly successful 27-year career in the Air Force.

"People dancing all in the street
See the rhythm all in their feet
Life is good wild and sweet
Let the music play on..."
*(Lionel Richie ~ Dancing in The Streets)*

The military was a great fit for me and I soon found myself on the fast track. In 1980, I was sent to the Pentagon in Washington D.C. I was a young, fast-moving, Lieutenant Colonel married to my career working 12 hour days and spending most Saturdays at the Pentagon. One dark, bitterly cold, Washington, D.C. winter morning as I drove to work, I heard Harry Chapin's "Cats in the Cradle" on the car radio and realized that my career had become more important to me than my family. That morning, I made a commitment to myself that I would value my family more than my career and make decisions that benefitted them more than myself. "Cats in the Cradle" was a turning point that put my life back into balance.

In 1980, I made the right decision for the right reasons... putting my family first. Now at 63 years old, my wife and I love each other more today than we did when we first met over 42 years ago. We have two grown and married children who are extremely successful. They are our best friends and they make us proud each and every day because of the people they have become. It all started with a song by Harry Chapin!

"When ya' comin' home Dad?
I don't know when but we'll get together then, son
Ya' know we'll have a good time then"
*(Harry Chapin ~ Cat's In The Cradle)*

My career, both past and present, requires much travel. As a result, I have become an expert at coping with the challenges that come from spending long hours in airports waiting for delayed flights or heading home at 10 pm on a three hour flight after a long business trip. That's when I pull out my iPod, plug in the studio-quality earbuds, and unleash some of the greatest music of all time. It's not the time for Simon and Garfunkel, Barry Manilow or James Taylor if your batteries need recharging. Instead, pull up some Jimmy Buffett, The Eagles, The Beatles or Three Dog Night. If it's a double shot of espresso that you need, then crank up The Doobie Brothers, Crosby, Stills, Nash & Young, The Stones, or The Who. Even better, dare to hit the play button on your "Best of the Best Classic Rock" playlist. If there is any doubt that music triggers the feel-good, mood-elevating, endorphins in your brain just try this little trick the next time you have miles to go but just can't seem to stay focused or keep your eyes open. Marathon runners talk about the "runner's high" after about 16 miles into the marathon. Make no mistake, great music can have the exact same effect on you without having to break a sweat!

"Well it seems that when I travel
And I'm out there on the road
The freedom I need is the freedom I leave
In my good time rock and roll

There's a healing in those guitars
And a spirit in the song
No matter what condition your rhythm is in
The message goes on and on

Music is the doctor...
Music is the doctor of my soul"
*(The Doobie Brothers ~ Doctor)*

So why did I write about the music of the 60's and 70's? Because music inspires me, music makes me feel alive, music brings back long-forgotten memories, and music changed my life.

That's how music affected my life, how has it affected yours?

*Disclaimer:*   While every effort has been made to properly attribute the lyrics to the original artist and album, in some cases, the song may also have been recorded by another artist. While the author attempted to be as comprehensive as possible during his search of over 170 artists and 1200 song lyrics, there are undoubtedly meaningful lyrics from other songs that may have been overlooked.  Readers are welcomed and encouraged to email the author with additional excerpts from lyrics which will be incorporated in the next edition of the book.

# The Rolling Stones

PRPhotos.com

# Putting It In Perspective

**"The Times They Are a-Changin'"**
*(Bob Dylan – The Times They Are a-Changin')*

# The 60's and 70's

## Events That Shaped the Music of the Times
## And Made It Timeless

# The 1960's

A convergence of cultural, political, and social upheaval marked the 1960's, resulting in a decade of unprecedented change. The Civil Rights movement led by Dr. Martin Luther King laid the foundation for the advancement of racial equality for African Americans. President John F. Kennedy challenged America to put a man on the moon by the end of the decade in response to the "space race" with the Soviet Union. The emergence of a counter-culture and the social revolution that followed brought liberal attitudes, demands for greater individual freedoms, and the desire to break free from traditional societal norms. The generation that grew up during the 60's rebelled against post WW II conservative values and is best remembered for the resulting hippie and drug cultures, the sexual revolution, the anti-war movement, radical student-lead protests, and the demand for more freedoms for women and minorities.

The first of the Baby Boomers graduated from high school in 1964 and from college in 1968. Not coincidentally, the rise of the counter-culture and the challenges to traditional societal norms came between 1963 and 1971. The US involvement in the

Vietnam war began in 1964 and peaked with the Tet Offensive from January to September 1968. President John F. Kennedy was assassinated on November 22, 1963, Dr. Martin Luther King was assassinated on April 4, 1968, and on July 21, 1969 Neil Armstrong became the first man to walk on the moon.

## The Civil Rights Movement

The Civil Rights Movement grew out of a century of grassroots efforts in a long struggle for equal rights for African Americans with the goal of abolishing segregation and racial discrimination and restoring equal suffrage in Southern states. The National Association for the Advancement of Colored People (NAACP) and the Urban League joined other organizations in employing legal, political, judicial, economic, and legislative means to help African Americans gain full citizenship rights. The Reverend Martin Luther King, Jr., and his colleagues in the Southern Christian Leadership Congress (SCLC) began a crusade of civil disobedience and nonviolent resistance beginning with the Montgomery Bus Boycott in 1955, spreading through sit-ins, marches, and demonstrations which ultimately resulted in the passage of the Civil Rights Act of 1964 and the Voting Rights Act in 1965. The Black Power Movement emerged in 1966 with the goal of expanding the aims of the Civil Rights Movement to include economic and political self-sufficiency as well as racial dignity.

## "The Great Society"

The Great Society was a set of domestic programs, including some initiatives carried over from John F. Kennedy's "New Frontier" that was proposed and enacted during Lyndon Johnson's presidency. In many ways, The Great Society resembled the "New Deal" domestic agenda of Franklin D. Roosevelt, but differed sharply in the types of programs enacted. The two main goals of The Great Society's social reforms were the elimination of poverty and racial injustice which resulted in massive new spending programs that addressed education, medical care, urban problems, and transportation. President Johnson's success was largely due to the Democratic landslide in the 1964 election that brought an influx of new liberals to Congress. While many of the original programs have been eliminated, some including Medicare, Medicaid and federal education funding continue today.

## The Vietnam War

The Vietnam War, also known as the Vietnam Conflict, occurred in Vietnam, Laos, and Cambodia from 1959 to April 30, 1975 and resulted in the death of 58,159 US soldiers. The war was fought between communist North Vietnam, supported by its communist allies, and South Vietnam, supported primarily by the United States who deployed combat units in 1965 to prevent a communist takeover of South Vietnam. US involvement peaked in 1968 at the time of the Tet Offensive. In April 1975, North Vietnam captured Saigon and a year later, North and South Vietnam were reunified. The war had a major impact on US politics, culture, and foreign relations. Americans were deeply divided over the US government's justification for, and conduct during the war. Opposition to the war contributed to the counter-culture youth movement of the 1960s.

## Transformational events of the 1960's include...

- The Cold War
- The Civil Rights Movement
- The Vietnam War

- James Meredith, an African-American student, is escorted by US Marshals to begin classes at the University of Mississippi (September 30, 1962)
- The Cuban Missile Crisis (October 16-28, 1962)
- President John F. Kennedy unveils the Apollo program in 1962 resulting in a technology explosion brought on by the "space race" and America's commitment to land a man on the moon before the end of the decade
- The assassination of JFK (November 22, 1963)
- The Beatles make their first live US appearance on the Ed Sullivan Show (February 9, 1964)
- The "Great Society" is unveiled by President Lyndon Johnson (May 22, 1964)
- At 35 years old, Dr. Martin Luther King, Jr. becomes the youngest person to ever be awarded the Nobel Peace Prize (December 10, 1964)
- US combat troops are deployed to South Vietnam in 1965
- "The Pill" becomes available to married women in America in 1965 and unmarried women in 1972
- President Johnson signs the Voting Rights Act of 1965 (August 6, 1965)
- The hippie / "free love" culture of the San Francisco "Flower Children"
- LSD and the drug culture
- The Black Panther Party is formed in Oakland, California on October 15, 1966 by Huey P. Newton and Bobby Seale
- The anti-war, protest movement
- The rise of the militant Students for a Democratic Society (SDS) and its pursuit of a "new left" political philosophy

- 100,000 young people from around the world gather at San Francisco's Haight-Ashbury district, at Berkeley, and other San Francisco Bay Area cities for "The Summer of Love" hippie experience (Summer 1967)
- Dissention within the Democratic Party over opposition to the Vietnam War forces President Lyndon Johnson not to seek reelection for a second term as President (March 31,1968)
- Dr. Martin Luther King is assassinated (April 4, 1968)
- Robert Kennedy is assassinated (June 5, 1968)
- Riots at the 1968 Democratic National Convention in Chicago organized and led by the SDS
- Tommie Smith (Olympic Gold Medal, 200m) and John Carlos (Olympic Bronze Medal, 200m) raise black-gloved fists in a "Black Power Salute" during the playing of the National Anthem at the 1968 Mexico City Olympic Games (October 1968)
- The Chicano movement lead by LULAC (League of United Latin American Citizens) and MALDEF (Mexican American Legal Defense and Education Fund) gains national recognition and power
- The emergence of the feminist and environmental movements
- Neil Armstrong walks on the moon (July 21, 1969)
- Woodstock (August 15-18, 1969)   Need I say more?
- Sesame Street featuring Big Bird, Kermit the Frog, and Bert & Ernie appears for the first time on PBS Television (November 10, 1969)

# The Music of the 60's

The music of the 60's reflected the culture of the times and was as diverse in style as it was in its message. *Folk and Folk Rock*, led by Bob Dylan, Joan Baez, Donovan, and groups such as The Mamas and the Papas enjoyed its greatest popularity in the early to mid 60's. *Soul/Motown* music led by groups such as The Temptations and The Supremes along with individual artists like James Brown, Aretha Franklin and Marvin Gaye enjoyed mainstream popularity from 1963 through the early 70's. The *"British Invasion"* lead by The Beatles, The Rolling Stones, and Rod Stewart, along with numerous other groups such as The Dave Clark 5, The Animals, and The Kinks shared the spotlight with Motown during that same period and brought with it a fresh, new style of rock music. *Rock* (not to be confused with "Rock and Roll") featured artists and groups such as The Doors, Janis Joplin, and Lynyrd Skynyrd. *Psychedelic Rock* with artists such as Jimi Hendrix, Jefferson Airplane, Pink Floyd, and the Grateful Dead emerged in the late 60's and early 70's and were heavily influenced by the drug culture (especially LSD) and the hippie movement.

The 60's was a hell of a decade if you loved music!

"We met as soul mates
On Parris Island
We left as inmates
From an asylum
And we were sharp
As sharp as knives
And we were so gung-ho
To lay down our lives

And who was wrong?
And who was right?
It didn't matter in the thick of the fight"
*(Billy Joel ~ Goodnight Saigon)*

# The 1970's

The progressive social trends of the late 60's continued into the 1970's and grew into more well defined and better-organized movements. The hippie culture faded by the mid 70's as the Vietnam War drew to a close. At the same time, opposition to nuclear weapons, advocacy for world peace, and hostility toward the government grew even more vocal. The environmental movement and green revolution came of age as did the demand for women's equality. The 70's were punctuated by the continued exponential growth of technology, and growing tensions within the Middle East. Of equal or perhaps even greater significance was a US economy stressed to the near breaking point resulting from a combination of internal and external economic forces including Middle Eastern oil embargos, a US stock market crash, and historically high inflation and unemployment rates.

## The Economy

The 1970's was the worst decade for the American economy since the Great Depression and in many ways equals the 2008-2009 US economic crises. The cost of the Vietnam War strained the US budget as did the "Great Society" which brought with it an unprecedented rise in domestic spending. Dramatic increases in oil prices also affected the retail sector leading to higher prices for both goods and services. Combined, these economic factors contributed to a period of inflation and a rise in interest rates never before seen in America. Between 1900 and 1970 inflation averaged 2.5%. During the 1970's, inflation averaged 6% topping out at 13.3% in 1979. The latter half of the 70's saw both inflation and unemployment steadily rise leading to double digit interest rates averaging over 12% and finally peaking at an historic high of 21.5% in December 1980. This period of stagflation resulted in a "misery index" (the sum of the unemployment rate and inflation rate) of 21.98% in 1980 – the last year of Jimmy Carter's Presidency. These factors together with a budget deficit of over $66 billion and a 10.8% unemployment rate led to a sharp recession in the early 80's.


# 1973 Oil Crisis

In October 1973 the Organization of Arab Petroleum Exporting Countries (OAPEC which included Arab members of OPEC, plus Egypt and Syria) announced an oil embargo in response to the US decision to re-supply the Israeli military during the Yom Kippur war. At the same time, OPEC oil ministers voted to use "oil as a weapon" and began to artificially set the price of oil to raise world oil prices. In early November, OPEC cut oil production an additional 25%. A gallon of gasoline cost $0.38 in May 1973 but by June 1974, the average price per gallon rose 43% to $0.55 a gallon putting additional pressure on an already stressed US economy.


# 1973-1974 Stock Market Crash

The 8th worst bear market in US history began on January 11, 1973 and extended for over 694 days (the third longest running bear market) resulting in a decline of 45% in the US stock market. By comparison, the 2008 bear market is the 11th worst in history lasting 406 days accompanied by a 41% drop in market value. In the two years between 1972 and 1974, the American economy slowed from 7.2% real GDP growth to a negative 2.1%. At the same time, inflation jumped from 3.4% in 1972 to 12.3% in 1974. Compounded by the 1973 oil crisis, the New York Stock Exchange Dow Jones Industrial Average lost over 45% of its value between Jan 11, 1973 and December 6, 1974. During one six week period alone, New York Stock Exchange shares lost over $97 billion in value.

# Events that shaped the decade of the 70's

- Four students are shot and killed and 11 more injured by National Guardsmen at Kent State University (May 4th, 1970)
- The first Earth Day is celebrated on April 22, 1970
- Munich Massacre – Eight Palestinian terrorists belonging to the Black September organization take 11 Israeli athletes hostage at the 1972 Munich Olympic Games resulting in the death of all eleven athletes and all but two of the terrorists (September 5, 1972)
- Apollo 17 -- the last man walks on the moon (December 11, 1972)
- The Vietnam era draft ends; the US military transitions to an "All Volunteer Force" (June 1973)
- Egypt and Syria attack Israel on Yom Kippur (October 6, 1973)
- The 1973 Middle East oil embargo
- 1973-1974 stock market crash
- The national maximum speed limit is reduced to 55 mph (Jan 2, 1974)
- President Nixon resigns becoming the only President to ever resign from office (August 9, 1974)
- The Vietnam War ends (April 30, 1975)
- The Carter Presidency (Jan 20, 1977 to Jan 20, 1981)
- The Iranian Hostage Crisis – Iranian militants occupy the US Embassy in Tehran holding embassy staff captive for over 444 days (November 4, 1979 to January 20, 1981)
- 21% interest rates
- The first integrated circuits, lasers, microprocessors, and fiber optics

- The first pocket calculator becomes available to the public

## Music of the 70's

Lead by such legendary artists as Elton John, James Taylor, Carole King, Billy Joel, The Eagles, Fleetwood Mac, and America, the 1970's saw the rise of *Soft Rock* which lasted throughout the decade. *Motown/Soul* underwent a transformation back to its rhythm and blues *(R&B)* roots with artists such as Stevie Wonder, Barry White, Lou Rawls and Earth, Wind & Fire. By the middle of the decade, various trends were vying for popular success. *Pop-Funk*, led by Sly & the Family Stone and *Glam Rock* led by David Bowie enjoyed some success. *Light Progressive-Rock* bands like Kansas, Journey, Chicago and Styx had long-running popularity. *Disco* dominated the charts (especially The Bee Gees) during the last few years of the decade but died a sudden death by the early 80's. *Punk Rock* featuring groups such as the Ramones, Depeche Mode and The Sex Pistols eventually transformed itself into *New Wave* which gained some momentum in the late 70's but more so into the 80's.

The *Rock* sound of the late 1960's became more hard-edged and gained even greater popularity. A few *Heavy Metal* bands like KISS attracted some mainstream attention in the 70's. Led Zeppelin became a worldwide phenomenon while former psychedelic rockers like Pink Floyd and The Steve Miller Band developed different musical styles and philosophical lyrics. Other influential and popular rock bands during the latter part of the 70's include Aerosmith, Van Halen, and Australian band AC/DC that all found further success well into the 80's.

Towards the end of the decade, traditional *Country Music* evolved into *Country-Rock* gaining mainstream popularity with the success of bands such as Lynyrd Skynyrd and The

Allman Brothers Band. The more contemporary Country style created by the group Alabama continues to influence Country musicians today and is what has made Country music today's most dominant genre.

"Against the wind
We were runnin' against the wind
We were young and strong, we were runnin'
Against the wind"
(Bob Seger ~ Against the Wind)

# Generations

## Why the Music of the 60's and 70's Is Timeless And Is as Popular Today as It Was 40 Years Ago

**Question:** What do the following artists have in common?

- The Eagles
- Rod Stewart
- Billy Joel
- The Rolling Stones
- Elton John
- Neil Diamond
- Bruce Springsteen
- Jimmy Buffett
- Sting/The Police
- Tina Turner
- Paul McCartney
- Aerosmith
- Cher
- Fleetwood Mac

## Answer:

1. All are icons in the music industry
2. They launched their musical careers in the 60's and 70's
3. In the past seven years (since 2001) all of these artists have had at least one Top 10 grossing US concert tour*

- In five of the past seven years, over half of the Top 10 highest-grossing US concert artists have come from this list*
- Eight of these artists have had a Top 10 grossing US concert tour in at least three of the past seven years – Elton John has been in the Top 10 six of the past 7 years!*
- The highest-grossing concert tour of all time was the Rolling Stones' 2005 "A Bigger Bang Tour"
- Stevie Wonder holds the record for the highest-grossing single concert raking in over $1.5m on October 3rd, 2008
- Eight of the Top 10 all-time highest-grossing worldwide concert tours are from 60's and 70's artists including The Rolling Stones, Bruce Springsteen, The Eagles, Pink Floyd, Cher and Tina Turner

4. **They are all Baby Boomers!**

\* Pollstar.com

In the past ten years, many 60's and 70's musical groups have launched reunion tours. Some may have lost their fortunes in the dot-com crash in the late 90's or they simply miss the thrill of performing. Others realize that even at age 50 or 60, they still have it in them to do what they love most... pursue their life's passion for entertaining people with great music. Either way, we are the beneficiaries of their decisions to dig out their guitars and get back up on stage. In addition to the previously listed well-known groups, artists such as The Doobie Brothers, James Taylor, Crosby, Stills Nash & Young, Orleans, and Stevie Wonder have had national or limited-engagement concert tours while others have performed in highly publicized "One Night Only" concerts. My wife and I have been to many of these concerts and I quickly noticed that they draw an eclectic mix of fans spanning across three generations. As you sit in an arena waiting for the show to begin and watch as 18,000 people take their seats, there are 20-30 year old Gen Y'ers, 30-44 year old Gen X'ers as well as 45+ Baby Boomers. Most of the premium, front row seats are filled not with Boomers, but fans in their 20's and 30's who stand throughout the concert and know the words to all of the songs. They are drawn to the music as much as we were the first time we attended a Rolling Stones, Beatles, Rod Stewart, Temptations, or James Brown concert 35 years ago. The only difference... back then, their hair was long and dark and they had flat stomachs – did we ever look like that? While these rockers are not as young as they once were (don't turn your binoculars on Keith Richards!), they are as good once as they ever were!

Boomers love the music because we grew up with it. The events of the 60's and 70's shaped our lives and music became a part of who we are today. When you listen to your iPod or go to a concert, it brings back memories of a simpler time in life. Regardless of your mood, the music puts a smile on your face and for a brief moment, lets you feel like you are 20 years old again. But music means different things to different people.

Our Gen X kids were born between 1964 and 1980 and most grew up before cable TV, Sirius Satellite Radio, iPods, or CD's were available. We generally kept our kids on a short leash. They spent a lot of time at home so the music that we listened to was the music that our kids also listened to growing up. I have to smile when we visit our grown, married, Gen X children and hear them listening to Billy Joel, James Taylor, Elton John, Sting and Jimmy Buffett or I see them put on an Eagles or Bee Gees concert DVD after dinner. They still listen to old CDs from a few 1980's and 90's artists such as Madonna, REM, Hootie and the Blowfish, and Erasure but there's no KISS, Marilyn Manson, Sid Vicious and The Sex Pistols, or Best of Menudo playing!

Generation Y (also known as the Millennial or Internet Generation) was born from the early 1980's to the late 90's. Gen Y grew up listening to Grunge, Rap, Hip-Hop, Gangsta Rap, Techno, and Alternative Rock. Late 90's Pop featured artists such as Britney Spears and Christina Aguilera as well as more traditional "boy-bands" such as The Backstreet Boys, 98 Degrees, and N'Sync. Gen Y didn't grow up listening to classic rock at home but they have been exposed to it everyday as they walk through the mall, ride an elevator, or go out to their favorite restaurant. The next time you're out, listen to the music playing in stores, restaurants, and outdoor malls and you'll find that much of it comes from the 60's and 70's. Most metropolitan areas have at least two or three radio stations that play classic rock 24/7 while Direct TV and Sirius Satellite Radio have stations devoted exclusively to music from the 60's, 70's and 80's. Gen Y'ers saw Stevie Wonder, Bruce Springsteen, and Aretha Franklin perform at the 2009 Presidential Inauguration and they have seen The Eagles, Elton John, Rod Stewart, and other concert tours on HDTV. For those in their 20's who are hearing it for the first time, the music of the 60's and 70's is fresh and new and they like it. They like the sound, the diverse musical styles, and they can relate to the messages and the stories intertwined within the music... something that they cannot find in contemporary music (with the noted exception of Country Music). Twenty years from now, will Generation Y remember MC Hammer, Tone Loc, Vanilla Ice, Tupac Shakur, Britney Spears, or Justin Timberlake? Will they still have any of their old CDs? My bet's on The Eagles and Bruce Springsteen!

Bottom line... the music of the 60's and 70's is timeless because it has both style and substance and because 76 million Baby Boomers grew up listening to it and still do. The music sparks the imagination with its stories and its messages. It talks about growing up, finding love, raising a family, living life, and confronting war, racial injustice, and other social issues. Perfect harmony makes the music easy to listen to while the rhythm and beat makes it even easier to dance to.

The most listened-to genre today is Country Music. The reason is simple. As mentioned in the introduction, Country Music went through a transformation in the 1980's and became mainstream as a result of a more contemporary sound. But in the process of loosing the twangy voices, banjoes, fiddles, and steel guitars, country artists never gave up their working class, pick-up truck-drivin', gun totin', hard-drinkin' and tender-lovin' roots. Today's artists such as Toby Keith, Montgomery Gentry, Brad Paisley, Kenny Chesney, and Alan Jackson are story tellers painting vivid pictures of real life situations and encounters. You may not be into Country Music but do yourself a favor and listen to Brad Paisley's "On-Line"; spark your imagination with Toby Keith's "Beer for My Horses"; or close your eyes and go back to summer vacations growing up when you listen to Kid Rock's "All Summer Long." Country artists continue to talk about family, patriotism, love of the land and living a simple life. Jimmy Buffett is still riding a 35 year tide of success because his music has a message... some serious but most of it whimsical and fun. Who can't imagine themselves living a laidback, Caribbean life style, drinking a margarita on a beach out of cell phone's reach when you listen to one of his songs? There's no doubt that Jimmy's music, along with Country Music, can take the listener to an imaginary place and give them a way to escape the stress of everyday life even if just for a brief moment while sitting in traffic on the early morning commute.

In the end, everyone wants the same thing from their music... to be entertained, to be reminded of special moments in our lives, to help us escape from the stress of everyday life, and to make us smile and be happy. The music of the 60's and 70's has been doing that for the past 40 years affecting three distinct generations in much the same way.

"Here is a little song I wrote
You might want to sing it note for note
Don't worry be happy"
*(Bobby McFerrin ~ Don't Worry Be Happy)*

# FYI

## Baby Boomers*

There are 76-78 million Baby Boomers who were born between 1946 and 1964 (45 to 63 years old in 2009). The first of the "Boomers" graduated from high school in 1964 and from college in 1968. The last Boomers entered high school in 1978 and graduated from college in 1986. In 1964, Baby Boomers represented 40% of the US population and with over 76 million in their ranks, Boomers have shaped the society that we live in today.

The Boomers are generally split into two groups. Those born between 1946 and 1957 who are referred to as the Leading Edge Boomers and those born between 1958 and 1964 sometimes referred to as the Shadow Boomers. The birth of Baby Boomers peaked in 1957 with over 4,300,000 births. The Leading Edge boomers reached their late teens during the height of the Vietnam War, the defining historical event of the decade that shaped their views on society, government, and in fact, the world. For those born between 1946 and 1955, the draft ensured that most served at some point during the Vietnam War.

**Likes:** Working from home, staying in shape, grandkids, outdoor sports such as cycling and hiking, good food and wines, adventure vacations, and staying up with technology

**Dislikes:** The prospects of retiring and growing old

**Challenges:** Aging parents, reinventing themselves as they face the prospect of retirement, staying young and living longer, coping with economic uncertainty, and the sudden loss of retirement savings

**Defining events and trends:** Prosperity, television, suburbia, assassinations, Vietnam, the Civil Rights Movement, women's rights, the Cold War, women's liberation, and the space race

**Attitudes:** Optimism, teamwork, get the job done, loyal to career and employer, personal satisfaction, health and wellness, personal growth

**Personality:** Driven, workaholics, devoted to the family, respect for others, a high importance on honesty and values, helping others

# Generation X*

Generation X (Gen-X) includes 44-48 million who were born between 1964 and 1981 (28 to 44 years old in 2009). This generation represents the bottoming-out of American birth rates from 1965 to 1975 after the post-World War II baby boom. Generation X began asserting itself in the late 80's and 90's and encompasses far fewer people than the Baby Boom Generation, and has had less impact on popular culture. This entrepreneurial, tech-savvy group has driven most of the Internet's growth and its rapidly expanding application. Microsoft, Amazon, Google, Yahoo, MySpace, Dell, and countless other billion-dollar Tech companies were founded by American Gen X'ers. They also created 70% of the start-up companies in the 90's!

As young adults, Generation X drew media attention in the late 1980s and early 1990's, gaining a stereotypical reputation as apathetic, cynical, disaffected, street wise loners. By the mid 1990's Generation X'ers were accusing Baby Boomers of hypocrisy and a "greed is good" mentality while Boomers accused Generation X of being overeducated and underachieving slackers. Today, Generation X finds themselves as parents concerned with the impact of a weakened economy and their family's security in a post 9/11 world.

**Defining events and trends:** Watergate, stagflation, latchkey kids, single parents, MTV, AIDS, drugs, computers, The Challenger, Ronald Reagan, the fall of the Berlin Wall, the end of the Cold War, teen violence, Marilyn Manson, Columbine, Wall Street greed, and fast money
**Attitudes:** Diversity, global thinking, independence, informal, emphasis on family, dual incomes, day-care, self-reliant and pragmatic
**Personality:** Individualistic, risk-takers, skeptical, family-oriented, bosses as colleagues, focused on the job – not work hours, more impressed by personal style than designer price tags

# Generation Y*

Generation Y, also known as the Millennial Generation or the Internet Generation ("iGen") represents 72-76 million of the population, born after Generation X from roughly the early 1980s to the late 1990s (11 to 27 years old in 2009). Generation Y is the first generation to grow up fully immersed in a digital, Internet driven world. They are the children of older Generation X parents who had children at a young age or are children of younger Baby Boomers that had children in a second or third marriages resulting in 10 to 18-year gaps between children. The term "Echo Boomers" or "Second Baby Boom" is often used as a way to denote the population expansion that Generation Y represents. If the years 1980 to 2000 are used to define this group, then the size of Generation Y in the United States is approximately 76 million – roughly the same number of Baby Boomers. Because of this, there appears to be a tendency for this group to share common social views with Baby Boomers but cultural perspectives with Gen X who are their older cousins or siblings.

In a 2007 survey conducted for CareerBuilder.com, nearly half the respondents noted Generation Y's preference to communicate via blogs, IMs, and text messages rather than on the phone or face-to-face as preferred by Boomers and Gen X. Other surveys have confirmed that up to 34% of Gen Y'ers use websites as their primary source for news, 28% keep a blog, 44% read blogs, and 75% have Facebook accounts. A Gallup Poll revealed that Millennials show greater interest in family, religion, and community than Generation X and, unlike Boomers, they are more interested in making their jobs accommodate their family and personal lives. They want jobs with flexibility, telecommuting options, and the ability to go part-time or leave the workforce temporarily when children are in the picture.

**Defining events and trends:** Internet, school violence, Oklahoma City bombing, Title IX, *It Takes A Village*, multiculturalism, 9/11, off-shoring and outsourcing, underage drinking, recreational drugs, tattoos and body piercing, childhood obesity, "helicopter parents," the Gulf War, and the Iraq War
**Attitudes:** Over confident, independent, entitled, group-oriented, challenge authority including their parents, their teachers and their employers, seek attention and expect to be noticed
**Personality:** Poor communicators, demanding, impatient, energetic, high performance in the workplace but also high maintenance, expects instant gratification, positive feedback and recognition, prefers teamwork and collective action

# Pampered, Protected, and Enabled Trophy Kids (also known as "Tweens")

While today's children certainly fall within this general definition, the trend towards raising children without holding them accountable for their actions began in the late 1990's if not earlier. Some of Generation Y born in the latter half of the 1990's were influenced by the way society, parents and the schools treat children and the result is now being seen in the workplace. In general, Pampered, Protected, and Enabled Trophy Kids have grown up...

- Never being told "no"
- Always being told they're winners and ceremoniously awarded a gold medal even when their soccer team comes in last place
- Being protected by their parents
- Being told that they are never wrong and that its always someone else's fault
- Finding ways to manipulate the system and the easy way out (often facilitated by their "helicopter parents")
- Learning that it's easier to instant message or text friends than to have a real conversation with them
- Raised in a world where being "politically correct" takes precedence over doing what's right

Some schools have even banned saying the Pledge of Allegiance for fear that the words "One Nation Under God" will offend someone... and teachers can't use a red pen to mark incorrect answers on a test for fear that it might damage the child's fragile self-image.

How will this generation impact the future?  The book is yet to be written.


"I'm so confused by the things I read, I need the truth
But the truth is, I don't know who to believe
The left says yes, and the right says no
I'm in between and the more I learn
Well, the less I know"
*(Styx ~ Borrowed Time)*


*Note:  Generations are not defined by a formal process, but rather by demographers, the media, popular culture, market researchers, and members of the generation themselves. Thus, two people of the same birth year might identify themselves as Generation X, Generation Y, or something that follows Generation Y, whatever that might be.

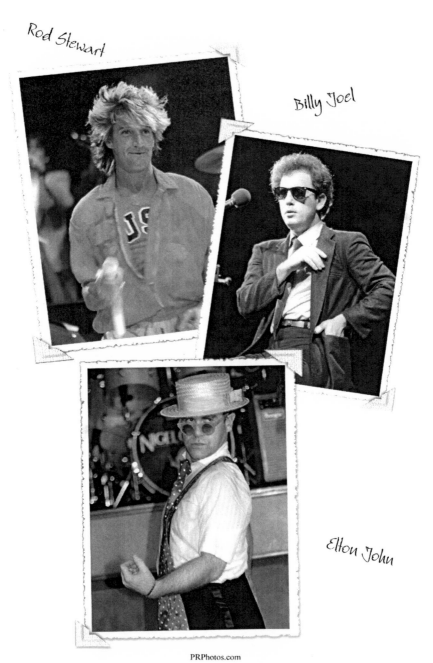

Rod Stewart

Billy Joel

Elton John

PRPhotos.com

40

# Chapters 1 - 6

## The Words You Don't Hear
## When You Listen to The Music

"And when my mind is free
You know a melody can move me
And when I'm feelin' blue
The guitar's coming through to soothe me

Thanks for the joy that you've given me
I want you to know I believe in your song
Rhythm and rhyme and harmony
You help me along, making me strong

Oh, give me the beat, boys, and free my soul,
I want to get lost in your rock and roll
And drift away"
*(Dobie Gray – Drift Away)*

# Chapter 1

# Growing Up and Finding Yourself

"When I was young, it seemed that
life was so wonderful,
A miracle, oh it was beautiful, magical
But then they sent me away to teach me
how to be sensible,
Logical, responsible, practical
And they showed me a world where
I could be so dependable,
Clinical, intellectual, and cynical

Won't you please, please tell me
what we've learned?
I know it sounds absurd
But please tell me who I am"
*(Supertramp ~ The Logical Song)*

# Introduction

"You gotta' bend a little one way or the other
You gotta' leave your mind open to discover"
*(Jimmy Buffett ~ You've Got to Bend a Little)*

I was born into a military family with parents that took raising a son was their #1 job. Before my teenage years, I had lived in Washington, D.C., Maine, Illinois, Texas, Japan, and Hawaii. Moving every two to three years teaches a kid to be adaptable, self-reliant, and self-confident. It also teaches you how to make friends quickly and to enjoy the moment... because it will change. I spent all my high school years in Washington, D.C. which was fortunate for me yet unusual as most "military brats" attended two or three high schools.

Growing up, I did all the things that normal kids do. I played little-league baseball, I was a Boy Scout, and I was a life guard at the neighborhood swimming pool. I learned to drive on a '61 VW Beetle when I was 16 and got my first speeding ticket that same year! I had a group of buddies and we did things that we didn't tell our parents about. It's amazing what can happen when you put a Cherry Bomb in a mail box or you throw a box of Tide laundry detergent in the courthouse fountain!

Dad taught me how to shoot a gun and I recall many bitterly cold mornings sitting on a log in the Blue-Ridge Mountains waiting for an unsuspecting deer to show itself. While we never saw that illusive 12 point buck, to pass the time Dad described in vivid detail his experiences as a 20-year old, B-17 Bombardier in World War II. Under a pre-dawn canopy of stars so brilliant that you could reach out and touch them, Dad told me of his faith in God and talked to me about the facts-of-life. The quiet beauty of those starlit mornings is as clear in my memory today as it was almost 50 years ago.

Shooting came easy to me so I took a few pistol lessons and by the time I was 16, I was winning competitions against people two and three times my age. While practicing at Quantico, Virginia, home of the Marine Corps' elite Shooting Team, I caught the attention of the Marine marksmen. As a young man, I was in awe of this group of battle-seasoned Marines and my hero was a young Marine Captain who had won a Gold Medal at the 1960 Olympic Games. I noticed that my Marine Corps mentors were calm and deliberate, poised and confident, and they neither smoked nor drank alcohol except for an occasional beer after the last day of competition. They led by example and I eagerly followed because I wanted to be a winner just like them. While my classmates were breaking curfew and finding ways to get their hands on a 6-pack of beer, I spent many Friday nights in bed early because I had a shooting competition at 7:30 the next morning. Periodically the Marines would offer me unsolicited advice and their timing always seemed to be impeccable. I recall being frustrated with my shooting one afternoon and began to curse. Overhearing me, one of the Marines quietly said... "Just remember, cursing doesn't make you a man, it only shows your ignorance." I was embarrassed but it was great advice for a young and impressionable 17-year old.

"Now that you know who you are
What do you want to be?"
*(The Beatles ~ Baby You're a Rich Man)*

My Marine Corps mentors taught me well and by my last year in high school, I had set 33 national pistol records and was the National Junior Pistol Champion. I was recruited by The Ohio State University, awarded an athletic scholarship and three weeks after graduating from high school, my parents dropped me off at a mammoth, 12-story dormitory on campus in Columbus, Ohio. Leaving home and finding myself in a strange city and at a university with over 50,000 students would test my ability to adapt and make friends. Within a few weeks, I received a surprise call from my father on the dormitory pay phone telling me that he was being sent to NATO Headquarters in Paris, France and that he and my mother would be gone for the next four years. Over the Labor Day weekend, I went back to Washington and said goodbye to my parents not knowing when I would see them again. I was on my own!

My first college roommate was an Ohio State Varsity Football player. I still remember Coach Woody Hayes walking through the dorm and sitting on the edge of the bed talking to my roommate like a good father, encouraging him to write his mother. My roommate was in a fraternity which I knew little about since neither of my parents had been in a fraternity or sorority. After visits to the fraternity house and several weekends spent at my roommate's home near Cleveland, I knew that I needed the fraternity more than it needed me. Just before Christmas that year, I survived "hell week" – the right of passage into a fraternity – and became a member of Sigma Alpha Epsilon.

"Guidance counselor said
Your scores are anti-heroic
Computer recommends
Hard-drinking calypso poet"
*(Jimmy Buffett ~ If It All Falls Down)*

Over the next three years, I spent my summer vacations in Europe with Mom and Dad – not a bad place to spend the summer for a young college kid. Without e-mail, cell phones, or satellite communications, I had very little contact with my parents throughout the rest of the year so my fraternity brothers became my family. I would spend Thanksgiving, Easter, and other holidays with a "brother" who would invite me to his home. Some weekends were spent on a family farm just for the simple pleasure of a home cooked meal and a change of scenery.

I became a leader within the fraternity heading up a number of committees and serving as Social Chairman for two years and later as Vice President. As the Social Chairman, I was the "party planner" in charge of making weekends fun for 80 guys and their dates. I auditioned bands, toured sites for parties, and looked for other ways to make the fraternity house everyone's home away from home because it certainly was mine. That's when I developed my love for music and came to appreciate the joy that it can bring to people. Tunes like "Louie-Louie", Aretha Franklin's "Respect," or The Stones "Satisfaction" gave you a second wind on a Friday night after a long week of classes. Putting on a little Cat Stevens, James Taylor, or Carole King would mellow you out on Sunday night as you prepared for the coming week's midterms. I learned that you could change the mood of a party simply by the songs that the band played and in what order they played them in. My fraternity brothers and my music helped get me through my college years without my parents' guiding hand. But... suffice it to say that I didn't let my education get in the way of my fun!

"Thank you for the music, the songs I'm singing
Thanks for all the joy they're bringing
Who can live without it, I ask in all honesty
What would life be?
Without a song or a dance what are we?
So I say thank you for the music
For giving it to me"
*(Abba ~ Thank You for the Music)*

It was not too many years after graduating from college I began to realize that my place in life was not so much of my own doing but was the result of those who influenced me, either knowingly or unknowingly, as I was growing up and finding myself. My parents sacrificed for me and always wanted my life to be better and more successful than theirs had been. My core values – honesty, integrity, compassion, love, and service to others – are the same values that my parents displayed each and every day of their lives. As I grew into my teenage years and was certain that I knew more about life than my parents did, I was influenced by 12 to 18 extremely focused Marine Corps marksmen who were at least twice my age but who saw in me what I could not see in myself. As I went through my years in college, I came to appreciate the value of friendship and how true friends can fill certain holes in one's life. Equally important, I realized that you only get out of a friendship what you put into it. Growing up, I was fortunate to have caring parents, mentors to guide me, and friends to help me through lonely times.

"Oh, I get by with a little help from my friends
Going to try with a little help from my friends"
*(The Beatles ~ With a Little Help From My Friends)*


That's one of my life's experiences, now what's yours?


As you turn the page and begin to read excerpts from the lyrics of over 250 classic rock songs, it will quickly become apparent that many artists of the 60's and 70's expressed their own fears and frustrations of growing up and finding themselves through their lyrics. Influenced by the events of the 60's, many wrote of peace, harmony, and of the need for racial equality. Others wrote of an idealistic life, the need to be free, and to *"Love the One You're With"* (Crosby, Stills, Nash & Young). Everyone's growing-up experience is different, but in the end, we all face many of the same challenges – the evolving relationship with parents, being faced with moral and ethical decisions, dealing with peer pressure, the need to "fit in," and struggling to break away and become independent. Your children faced those same daunting challenges and their children will do the same. In many ways, it's a universal experience that links all generations together.

# Timeless Lessons
## on
# Growing Up and Finding Yourself

Well I grew up believin' I could do what I wanted to do
When I got a little older I found that it just wasn't true
*(John Mellencamp ~ American Dream)*

~

Sometimes I lie awake at night and wonder
Where my life will lead me
*(Jackson Browne ~ Sleep's Dark and Silent Gate)*

~

I have opened up my mind
To things I was afraid of
Done things I've never done before
Taken a chance and seen just what
The world is made of
Nothing is the same any more
*(Carole King ~ Welcome Home)*

~

I got nothing to do and all day to do it
I've no place to go and all night to get there
*(Styx ~ I've Got Too Much Time on My Hands)*

Well my soul checked out missin' as I sat listenin'
To the hours and minutes tickin' away
Just sittin' around waitin' for my life to begin
While it was all just slippin' away
*(Bruce Springsteen ~ Better Days)*

~

The boy's got brains
He just don't use em that's all
*(Paul Simon ~ Oh Marion)*

~

I listen to the wind
The wind of my soul
Where I'll end up, well I think
Only God really knows
*(Cat Stevens ~ The Wind)*

~

You say you want a revolution
Well you know
We all want to change the world
*(The Beatles ~ Revolution)*

~

Some of the simple things you see are all complicated
*(The Who ~ Substitute)*

~

Don't you understand what I'm tryin' to say
Can't you feel the fears I'm feelin' today
*(Barry McGuire ~ Eve of Destruction)*

Now a good friend of mine
Sat with me and he cried
He told me a story
I know he ain't lying

Said he went for a job
And the man said...
"Without an education
You might as well be dead"
(James Brown ~ Don't Be a Dropout)

~

Crazy notions fill your head,
You gotta' break all the records set
Push yourself until the end
But don't you ever give up on your dream
(Rod Stewart ~ Never Give Up on Your Dream)

~

'Cause they told me when I was younger
"Boy you're gonna' be President"
But just like everything else, those old crazy dreams
Just kinda' came and went
(John Mellencamp ~ Pink Houses)

~

I had to go 'cause I could see
I wasn't meant for poverty
The family ties were broken soon
I went off to find the moon
(Jimmy Buffett ~ There's Nothing Soft About Hard Times)

Ticking away the moments that make up a dull day
You fritter and waste the hours in an offhand way
Tired of lying in the sunshine staying home to watch the rain
You are young and life is long and there is time to kill today

And then one day you find ten years have got behind you
No one told you when to run, you missed the starting gun
*(Pink Floyd ~ Time)*

~

They said stay at home, boy, you gotta' tend the farm
Living in the city, boy, is going to break your heart
But how can you stay when your heart says no
How can you stop when your feet say go
*(Elton John ~ Honkey Cat)*

~

Well, the bigger the city, the brighter the lights
The bigger the dog, the harder the bite
*(Lynyrd Skynyrd ~ I Know a Little)*

~

There's nothing you can know that isn't known
Nothing you can see that isn't shown
Nowhere you can be that isn't where you're meant to be
There's nothing you can do that can't be done
*(The Beatles ~ All You Need is Love)*

~

I was living to run and running to live
Never worried about paying or even how much I owed
*(Bob Seger ~ Against the Wind)*

What he lacked in ambition
He made up with intuition
*(Jimmy Buffett ~ Cowboy in The Jungle)*

~

I am blinded by the light
Of God and truth and right
*(Paul Simon ~ Flowers Never Bend in The Rainfall)*

~

'Cause here there's lots of room for doing
The things you've always been denied
So look and gather all you want to
There's no one here to stop you trying
*(The Moody Blues ~Watching and Waiting)*

~

Time keeps on slippin', slippin', slippin',
Into the future
*(The Steve Miller Band ~ Fly Like an Eagle)*

~

There's always lots of things that we can see
We can be anyone we want to be
*(The Young Rascals ~ Groovin')*

I was born here in the city
With my back against the wall
Nothing grows and life ain't very pretty
No one's there to catch you when you fall

Somewhere out on that horizon
Far away from the neon sky
I know there must be somethin' better
And I can't stay another night
In the city
*(The Eagles ~ In The City)*

~

Little Leo is a friend of mine
We get some money and we buy a cheap wine
Sit on the corner and have a holiday
Hide the bottle when the cop goes by
Talk about women and lie, lie, lie
*(Billy Joel ~ Half a Mile Away)*

~

Time for me to fly
Oh, I've got to set myself free
*(REO Speedwagon ~ Time For Me To Fly)*

~

Lookin' back on when I was a little nappy-headed boy
Then my only worry was for Christmas what would be my toy
Even though we sometimes would not get a thing
We were happy with the joy that they would bring
I wish those days could come back once more
Why did those days ever have to go
I wish those days could come back once more
Why did those days ever have to go cause I loved 'em so...
*(Stevie Wonder ~ I Wish)*

Get your motor running
And head out on the highway
Looking for adventure
And whatever comes your way
*(Steppenwolf ~ Born To Be Wild)*

~

I was supposed to have been a Jesuit priest
or a Naval Academy grad
That was the way that my parents perceived me
Those were the plans that they had
*(Jimmy Buffett ~ We're the People Our Parents Warned Us About)*

~

How many years can a mountain exist
Before it's washed to the sea
How many years can some people exist
Before they're allowed to be free

The answer, my friend, is blowin' in the wind
The answer is blowin' in the wind
*(Bob Dylan ~ Blowin' In The Wind)*

~

I stopped into the courthouse
Had to pay some bills
Got talking with the judge
About the finer points of my driving skills
He said: "Son you only drive that way
Tryin' to get your thrills
But bear in mind your driver's license
Ain't never been no license to kill"
*(Crosby, Stills, Nash & Young ~ Drivin' Thunder)*

I rose above the noise and confusion
To get a glimpse beyond this illusion
*(Kansas ~ Carry On Wayward Son)*

~

Say it loud, I'm black and I'm proud
*(James Brown ~ Say It Loud, I'm Black and I'm Proud)*

~

T-shirts, cut-offs, and a pair of thongs
We've been having fun all summer long
Every now and then we hear our song
We've been having fun all summer long
*(The Beach Boys ~ All Summer Long)*

~

We are the young ones crying out
Full of anger, full of doubt
And we're breaking all of the rules
Never choosing to be fools
*(Peter Frampton ~ Breaking All The Rules)*

~

War has caused unrest in the younger generation
Induction, then destruction, who wants to die?
War has shattered many young man's dreams
Made him disabled, bitter and mean
*(The Temptations ~ War)*

There's a place in the world for the angry young man
With his working class ties and his radical plans
He refuses to bend, he refuses to crawl
He's always at home with his back to the wall
But his honor is pure and his courage as well
And he's fair and he's true but he's boring as hell
*(Billy Joel ~ Angry Young Man)*

~

Well now don't try to cook nothin' up
Brother you know you'll only wind up in your own stew
Just don't let nobody tell you
What you ought'a' do
*(Lynyrd Skynyrd ~ Ain't No Good Life)*

~

So you think your schooling's phony
I guess it's hard not to agree
You say it all depends on money
And who is in your family tree
*(Supertramp ~ Bloody Well Right)*

~

My Maserati
Does one eighty-five
I lost my license
Now I don't drive
*(The Eagles ~ Life's Been Good)*

So if I can, I'm gonna break from this prison
Gonna' get out and join in the fight
Take a chance on what I believe in
Win or lose, I know its right
*(Styx ~ High Time)*

~

But in the grey of the morning
My mind becomes confused
Between the dead and the sleeping
And the road that I must choose
*(The Moody Blues ~ Question)*

~

Remember a day before today
A day when you were young
Free to play alone with time
Evening never came
*(Pink Floyd ~ Remember a Day)*

~

When I think back on all the crap
I've learned in high school
It's a wonder I can think at all
Though my lack of education hasn't hurt me much
I can read the writings on the wall
*(Paul Simon ~ Kodachrome)*

~

And all the wondering and the stumbling
That goes hand-in-hand with change
The yearning, the earning was it all part of learning
Or am I still the same?
*(Rod Stewart ~ Only A Boy)*

Oh when you were young
Did you question all the answers?
Did you envy all the dancers?
Who had all the nerve
*(Crosby, Stills, Nash & Young ~ Wasted on the Way)*


~


I had to misbehave
I did things in reverse
Refused to wash or shave
I was horrid to my nurse
I got back what I gave
Which only made me worse
*(James Taylor ~ Mean Old Man)*


~


Every night I say a prayer in the hope that there's a heaven
And every day I'm more confused
as the saints turn into sinners
All the heroes and legends I knew as a child
have fallen to idols of clay
And I feel this empty place inside so afraid
that I've lost my faith

Show me the way, show me the way
Give me the strength and the courage
To believe that I'll get there someday
*(Styx ~ Show Me the Way)*

PRPhotos.com

# Chapter 2

# Falling In Love,
# Falling Out Of Love,
# And Finding True Love

"If I had a box just for wishes
And dreams that had never come true
The box would be empty
Except for the memory
Of how they were answered by you"
*(Jim Croce ~ Time in A Bottle)*

# Introduction

At Christmas, I never make a list of things to buy for my family. Instead, I set aside several nights or a weekend or two just to wander through my favorite stores and suddenly, something catches my eye... the perfect gift found! Usually it's something that the person never knew they wanted until they open it on Christmas morning and then wonder how they ever lived without it. Finding my true love was much the same as shopping for the perfect Christmas gift... I didn't really know what I was looking for, but when I least expected it, I found it.

During my first semester at Ohio State, I joined a fraternity and found myself constantly searching for a date for the next fraternity party, pre-football game brunch, formal Founder's Day dinner, or simply to go TGIF'n after classes on Friday. I met a young woman who sat next to me in the cafeteria (let's call her Jane) and we struck up a conversation. She was attractive and intelligent and a sophomore which made it kinda' cool for a new freshman. She was somewhat shy but Jane was "low maintenance" and easy to talk to. I soon found myself asking her to most, if not all, of the fraternity social events. While we had fun, Jane certainly took the pressure of having to find a new date every week. The weeks turned into months and the months turned into years. In June 1967, Jane graduated and was about to begin her teaching career as I jetted off to Europe to spend the summer with my parents.

I am an only child and the closest thing to a brother or sister I ever had was my cousin, Ann who was several years older than I. Ann, who was a nurse living in Boston, had never been to Europe so asked if she could tag along during my final visit to see my parents. Ann loved rock music and dancing as much as I did, so for six weeks, we hit just about every disco and dance club from London to Paris and Belgium to Berlin. During that summer, we talked about growing up, the uncertain life that lay ahead, and we had a running conversation about my three-year relationship with Jane. By the end of the summer, I finally admitted to myself that while Jane was sweet, kind and caring, we didn't have much in common. In the end, it was more of a sense of security than true love that had kept us together for the past three years. I knew that when I returned, Jane was expecting an engagement ring and that if I didn't break up with her, then I would spend the rest of my life living with someone who I didn't truly love. I'm a sensitive guy so walking into her apartment after being gone the past three months and telling Jane that I wasn't in love with her was one of the most difficult things I had ever done. It was painful at the time but it was possibly the best decision I have ever made in my life.

"Nothin' real comes overnight
You weren't sure if it felt right"
*(Carole King ~ Love Makes the World)*

The next few weeks found me once again searching for dates for the next fraternity party. I was more self confident now so finding a date was not the daunting task it once was. A week into the new school year, I was at a presentation in a campus auditorium and happened to sit next to a young lady who was strikingly beautiful. Tall, slender, dark hair, and a smile that would light up a room from a mile away, she also had a personality and a certain energy that made you feel like you had known her all your life. I asked her out, she said yes, and several nights later, we were sharing a pizza after a study date. Study date... is that an oxymoron? From that first, chance encounter on a Sunday afternoon in October, there was something magical and captivating about Susann. She was strong, yet sensitive. She was enthusiastic, adventuresome, and had a zeal for living life. Despite hardships growing up, her cup was always half full and she genuinely appreciated even the most simple gestures of kindness and love. Susann had an indescribable quality about her that made me feel like I had never felt before. She was perfect! She was The one... and I knew it after our second date. I could only hope that she would eventually feel the same way about me. While she was dating someone from a rival fraternity, I was persistent, and within a week or two, we were studying together almost every night and having dinners at my apartment.

"I love the colorful clothes she wears
And the way the sunlight plays upon her hair
I hear the sound of a gentle word
On the wind that lifts her perfume through the air

I'm pickin' up good vibrations
She's giving me excitations"
(The Beach Boys ~ Good Vibrations)

Walking home from a Saturday afternoon football game just three weeks after we first met, we stopped into the jewelry store and picked out an engagement ring. She didn't say no, so I took that as a yes. It would take some time to order the ring so I gave her my fraternity pin and two months later on Christmas morning, I formally proposed and gave her the ring. Eight months later, following our graduation from Ohio State, we were married during a modest military wedding. After a brief and inexpensive honeymoon, we drove to San Antonio, Texas in our new Pontiac GTO for my first assignment in the Air Force, and the first of what would be many great adventures to follow. It took three years to be honest enough with myself to admit that I didn't love Jane. It took me a matter of days to know that Susann was the only person in this world I wanted to share the rest of my life with. There is a God in heaven because He made her feel the same way about me!

That was 41 years ago, and while we didn't know then how life would turn out, today we wouldn't change a thing. We'd do it all over again – exactly the same. As I began writing this book, Susann and I came to realize how music has been intertwined throughout our lives together. We share the same memories of people and places when we hear certain songs. I took Susann to a James Brown concert soon after we met and anytime we hear the "Godfather of Soul" we think about those early days as we were falling in love. There were some great dance clubs in San Antonio in the late 60's and Friday nights would find us along with several of our friends dancing until the club closed and we were finally asked to leave. Anytime we hear "Hey Jude" by the Beatles, we are immediately transported back to 1970 at a club called "The Pit" in San Antonio. Several years later, we were dancing to "Proud Mary" by Creedence Clearwater Revival in a small quonset hut turned-Officers' Club at Incirlik Air Base in Adana Turkey. Fifteen years later, we were once again dancing to "Hey Jude," "Proud Mary," "Rubber Band Man" by the Spinners, and "Ain't Too Proud to Beg" by The Temptations at a dance club on Waikiki Beach with three other couples who enjoyed the music as much as we did.


**"You made me so very happy**
**I'm so glad you**
**Came into my life"**
*(Blood, Sweat and Tears ~ You Made Me So Very Happy)*

What has this got to do with finding your soul mate? Soon after beginning their lives together, a couple comes to the stark realization that finding the love of your life is actually the easy part. The hard part is becoming soul mates who willingly share life's everyday challenges, who revel in the good times together, and who cope with the tough times as one.

"We've been through thick and thin, and back again
And we can endure love's sweet pain
Remember, starting the fire is easy
The hardest part is learning how to keep the flame"
*(Stevie Nicks ~ Love's A Hard Game To Play)*

A couple becomes soul mates and best friends when they openly communicate with each other, holding nothing back; when they give and ask nothing in return; when trust and respect becomes as deep as their love; and when bringing a smile to the face of your lover and best friend gives you more pleasure than anything money can buy. Sharing common interests and learning to enjoy your partner's passions even though they may not match your own is what brings your lives together; building a rock-solid foundation that helps you face all of the uncertainties that life will throw your way. Some husbands and wives play golf together, others enjoy hiking and mountain biking, or taking adventure vacations together. Some couples wait with anxious anticipation for the start of the symphony season, while others share a passion for wine and can't wait to return to Napa Valley to explore their favorite wineries. Susann and I share a wide variety of interests including a common love of the music from the 60's and 70's. We never pass up a chance to seek out a new local band and hit the dance floor when they play The Beatles, the Stones, The Temptations and "All Night Long" by Lionel

Richie.  We play "name that tune" while driving in the car and often talk about shared memories and experiences that our common love of music has given us. Becoming soul mates, not just lovers and friends or man and wife, means living two lives as one.  Rod Stewart said it best...


"You're in my heart, you're in my soul
You'll be my breath should I grow old
You are my lover, you're my best friend
You're in my soul"
*(Rod Stewart ~ You're In My Heart)*


I learned that you can't go looking for love.  Instead, love finds you... sometimes in mysterious ways.  It's like finding that perfect Christmas gift.  You don't know what you're looking for but you'll know it when you see it.


That's one of my life's experiences, now what's yours?

# Timeless Lessons
on
# Falling In Love, Falling Out Of Love, Finding True Love

If I could make days last forever
If words could make wishes come true
I'd save every day like a treasure and then
Again, I would spend them with you
*(Jim Croce ~ Time In A Bottle)*


~


My love for you is immeasurable
My respect for you immense
You're ageless, timeless, lace, and fineness
You're beauty and elegance

You're a rhapsody, a comedy
You're a symphony and a play
You're every love song ever written
But honey what do you see in me
*(Rod Stewart ~ You're In My Heart)*


~


You fill up my senses
Like a night in the forest
Like the mountains in springtime
Like a walk in the rain
Like a storm in the desert
Like a sleepy blue ocean
You fill up my senses
Come fill me again
*(John Denver ~ Annie's Song)*

Now I know the secret, there is nothing that I lack
If I give my love to you, you'll surely give it back
*(Eric Clapton ~ Let It Rain)*

~

At least in my lifetime
I've had one dream come true
I was blessed to be loved
By someone as wonderful as you
*(KC and The Sunshine Band ~ Please Don't Go)*

~

You came upon a quiet day
You simply seemed to take your place
I knew that it would be that way
The minute that I saw your face
*(The Lovin' Spoonful ~ You Didn't Have to Be So Nice)*

~

You are sunshine, you are shadows
You are morning, you are night
You are hard times, you are good times
You are darkness, you are light
*(Captain & Tennille ~ The Way I Want to Touch You)*

~

I said I love you and that's forever
And this I promise from the heart
I could not love you any better
I love you just the way you are
*(Billy Joel ~ Just The Way You Are)*

I'm going to find myself a girl
Who can show me what laughter means
And we'll fill in the missing colors
In each other's paint-by-number dreams
*(Jackson Browne ~ The Pretender)*

~

It's a mystery
How the heart beats
How the sun shines
How our eyes meet
*(Bob Seger ~ It's a Mystery)*

~

You're a candle in the window
On a cold, dark winter's night
*(REO Speedwagon ~ Can't Fight This Feeling)*

~

Have I told you lately that I love you
Have I told you there's no one else above you
You fill my heart with gladness
Take away all my sadness
Ease my troubles, that's what you do
*(Rod Stewart ~ Have I Told You Lately That I Love You)*

~

Love is still a simple act of faith
And a faithful heart is always worth the wait
Gold don't rust, love don't lie
I'll be true 'til the day that I die
*(Neil Diamond ~ Gold Don't Rust)*

If you like Pina Coladas
And getting caught in the rain
If you're not into yoga
If you have half a brain
If you'd like making love at midnight
In the dunes on the Cape
Then I'm the love that you've looked for
Write to me and escape
*(Rupert Holmes ~ Escape – "The Pena Colada Song")*

~

Sweet wonderful you
You make me happy with the things you do
You make loving fun
And I don't have to tell you you're the only one
*(Fleetwood Mac ~ You Make Loving Fun)*

~

Woman I know you understand
The little child inside the man
*(John Lennon ~ Woman)*

~

How sweet it is to be loved by you
*(James Taylor ~ How Sweet It Is To Be Loved By You)*

~

But once inside a woman's heart
A man must keep his head
Heaven opens up the door
Where angels fear to tread
*(Bob Seger ~ Shame On the Moon)*

74

For once in my life I have someone who needs me
Someone I've needed so long
For once, unafraid I can go where life leads me
Somehow I know I'll be strong
For once I can touch what my heart used to dream of
Long before I knew someone warm like you
Would make my dream come true
*(Stevie Wonder ~ For Once In My Life)*

~

The first time ever I lay with you
And felt your heart beat close to mine
I thought our joy would fill the earth
And last 'till the end of time, my love
And last 'till the end of time
*(Roberta Flack ~ The First Time Ever I Saw Your Face)*

~

My love
There's only you in my life
The only thing that's bright
My first love
You're every breath that I take
You're every step I make
*(Lionel Richie & Diana Ross ~ Endless Love)*

~

Just the two of us
We can make it if we try
Just the two of us
Building castles in the sky
Just the two of us
You and I
*(Bill Withers ~ Just The Two Of Us)*

When I was young
I never needed anyone
And makin' love was just for fun
Those days are gone
*(Eric Carmen ~ All By Myself)*

~

All my life, without a doubt I give you
All my life, now and forever
'Till the day I die
You and I will share
*(America ~ All My Life)*

~

I'll build a stairway to heaven
I'll climb to the highest star
I'll build a stairway to heaven
'Cause heaven is where you are
*(Neil Sedaka ~ Stairway to Heaven)*

~

I'll give you all I've got to give if you say you love me too
I may not have a lot to give but what I got I'll give to you
I don't care too much for money, money can't buy me love
*(The Beatles ~ Can't By Me Love)*

~

The look of love
Is in your eyes
The look your smile can't disguise
And what my heart has heard
Takes my breath away
*(Dusty Springfield ~ The Look of Love)*

I'm standin' at the crossroads
Tryin' to read the signs
To tell me which way I should go
To find the answer
And all the time I know
Plant your love and let it grow.
*(Eric Clapton ~ Let It Grow)*

~

Some people never say the words 'I love you'
It's not their style to be so bold
Some people never say the words 'I love you'
But like a child they're longing to be told
*(Paul Simon ~ Something So Right)*

~

Lookin' out on the morning rain
I used to feel so uninspired
And when I knew I had to face another day
Lord it made me feel so tired
Before the day I met you
Life was so unkind
But you're the key to my peace of mind

'Cause you make me feel
Like a natural woman
*(Aretha Franklin ~ You Make Me Feel Like a Natural Woman)*

~

You're my first, my last, my everything
And the answer to all my dreams
You're my sun, my moon, my guiding star
My kind of wonderful, that's what you are
*(Barry White ~ You're My First, The Last, My Everything)*

Any kind of love without passion
That ain't no kind of lovin' at all
*(The Eagles ~ After The Thrill Is Gone)*

~

Love's a hard game to play
The heart's the price you pay
No matter what they say
Win or lose, no matter what they say
Love's a hard game to play
*(Stevie Nicks ~ Love's A Hard Game To Play)*

~

Say that you'll marry me
Sometimes carry me
And I will be there forever more for you
Promise you'll stay with me
We'll make some memories
And maybe a dream or two will come true
*(Neil Diamond ~ Marry Me)*

~

You and me for eternity, in love we'll always be
Young and free and naturally, the way it's gotta be
*(Hamilton, Joe Frank & Reynolds ~ Fallin' In Love)*

~

Someday when we're dreaming
Deep in love, not a lot to say
Then we will remember
The things we said today
*(The Beatles ~ Things We Said Today)*

You're everything I hoped for
You're everything I need
You are so beautiful
You are so beautiful to me
*(Joe Cocker ~ You Are So Beautiful)*

~

I know I can't express
This feeling of tenderness
There's so much I wanna' say
But the right words just don't come my way

I just know when I'm in your embrace
This world is a happy place
And something happens to me
That's some kind of wonderful
*(Carole King ~ Some Kind of Wonderful)*

~

Maybe you can tell me
How a love so right
Can turn out to be so wrong
*(The Bee Gees ~ Love So Right)*

~

I need you like the flower needs the rain
You know I need you, guess I'll start it all again
You know I need you like the winter needs the spring
You know I need you, I need you
*(America ~ I Need You)*

~

Some love is just a lie of the heart
The cold remains of what began with a passionate start
But that can't happen to us
Because it's always been a matter of trust
*(Billy Joel ~ A Matter of Trust)*

If a man could be two places at
One time, I'd be with you
Tomorrow and today
Beside you all the way
*(Bread ~ If)*

~

In the chilly hours and minutes
Of uncertainty, I want to be
In the warm hold of your loving mind
To feel you all around me
And to take your hand along the sand
Ah, but I may as well try and catch the wind
*(Donovan ~ Catch The Wind)*

~

Stay with me a while
Said you'd give me light
But you never told be about the fire
*(Fleetwood Mac ~ Sara)*

~

Baby, it's amazing just how wonderful it is
That the things we like to do are just the same
*(Hot Chocolate ~ Everyone's A Winner)*

~

Help me
I think I'm falling
In love too fast
It's got me hoping for the future
And worrying about the past
'Cause I've seen some hot, hot blazes
Come down to smoke and ash
*(Joni Mitchell ~ Help Me)*

Who knows how long I've loved you
You know I love you still
Will I wait a lonely lifetime
If you want me to--I will
*(The Beatles ~ I Will)*

~

They say in the end true love prevails
But in the end true love can't be some fairy tale
To say I'll make your dreams come true would be wrong
But maybe darlin', I could help them along
*(Bruce Springsteen ~ I Wanna' Marry You)*

~

You shared my dreams, my joys, my pains
You made my life worth living
And if I had to live my life over again
I'd spend each and every moment with you
*(The Commodores ~ Three Times a Lady)*

~

I was hightop shoes and shirt tails
Suzy was in pig tails
I know I loved her even then
You know my papa disapproved it
My mama boohooed it
But I told them time and time again
"Don't you know I was made to love her
Build a world all around her"
*(Stevie Wonder ~ I Was Made To Lover Her)*

Stevie Wonder

Jimmy Buffett

To view the entire photo album go to
**listentothemusiclyrics.com**

# Chapter 3

# Raising a Family

"Isn't she lovely
Isn't she wonderful
Isn't she precious
Less than one minute old

I never thought through love we'd be
Making one as lovely as she
But isn't she lovely

I can't believe what God has done
Through us he's given life to one
But isn't she lovely... made from love"
*(Stevie Wonder ~ Isn't She Lovely)*

# Introduction

"Teach your children what you believe in
Make a world that we can live in"
*(Crosby, Stills, Nash & Young ~ Teach the Children)*

In 1980, I was a young, fast-moving, Lieutenant Colonel with a wife, two young children and an 18% mortgage on a 2000 sq. ft. townhouse in Washington, D.C. I was assigned to the Pentagon and as with most Boomer's, I was married to my career working 12-hour days and spending many Saturdays in the Pentagon. One dark, bitterly cold, Washington, D.C. morning as I sat silently between two other guys in the backseat of our 5-man carpool, I first heard Harry Chapin's *"Cats in the Cradle"* on the car radio.

"My child arrived just the other day,
He came to the world in the usual way.
But there were planes to catch, and bills to pay,
He learned to walk while I was away"
*(Harry Chapin ~ Cat's in The Cradle)*

I fought back the tears and realized at that moment that I had lost sight of what was most important in life. Over time, I had become so caught-up with moving-up that I had lost touch with what was most important... my family. That morning, I made a commitment to myself that I would value my family more than my career and would start making decisions that benefitted them more than myself. Other than the occasional deadline or critical project that required some late-night work, I was home in time for dinner and spent Saturdays at soccer games, at dance or piano recitals, or walking leisurely through the Smithsonian with my family. No more briefcases brought home from the office to extend a 12-hour workday into 14 hours and no more missed birthdays or anniversaries. I was still focused and tenacious at work but when I was home, I was relaxed and enjoyed every moment with my family.

More than just attending soccer games and PTA meetings, I began to look for ways to spend quality time with my family. I had fond memories of family dinners when I was growing up. While everyone's life was being pushed and pulled, dinner was a time that the entire family would gather and talk about the day, seek advice, comment about the news, or simply enjoy each other's company. Twenty-five years later, I still remembered dinners as a special time growing up. If it made an impression on me then, could it not have the same affect on my family now? My wife and I enjoy cooking, so we began making Sunday dinners special. It became a team effort… everyone had input into the next week's menu… one week it could be lasagna, the next week it could be shrimp, or a simple homemade soup with homemade bread or maybe it was a special dessert that we had not had for a while. Sunday evenings found us all in the kitchen helping to prepare dinner, set the table and clean up afterwards. Regardless of the menu, Sunday dinners quickly became something that everyone looked forward to with great anticipation and a time to be enjoyed if not just for its shear simplicity.

Sunday nights were jam-packed with conversation about the events of the previous week and the challenges of the coming week. An important math test in school, Dad's budget briefing to the 3-Star General, Mom's conference with the parents of a troubled student, or the upcoming regional soccer tournament... there was always lots to talk about. One night, I casually mentioned the Carpenter's Creed that my father taught me – *"measure twice and saw once"* – and we all began to talk about its meaning. There was a real energy at dinner that night. Everyone had a point of view, everyone was engaged in the discussion, everyone listened, and everyone respected each other's opinions. From that night on, a quote became a part of our Sunday dinners and Cristy and Glen would write each weekly quote in a small notebook we gave them. In a few months, we began taking turns finding a quote for the coming week and leading the discussion. The kids took the challenge with enthusiasm each trying to out-do the other. Today, Cristy and Glen still have their quote books and every week or so, someone will email a quote that they want to share with the family. Cristy, a fast-track engineer with Raytheon Corporation, includes a weekly quote at the conclusion of her emails and Susann puts a weekly quote on the board for her students at school. A simple idea that has become a family tradition.

Quiet Sunday family dinners free from TV and other distractions provided the perfect opportunity to discuss subjects that are sometimes difficult to talk about with young people. Drug and alcohol use, premarital sex, picking friends, how to respond to certain difficult situations, inevitable challenges to one's honesty and integrity, and other critical life decisions that all kids are faced with. There were no lectures, no "do as I say" speeches. We had open and frank discussions in a relaxed and trusting environment where views were shared and respected. The preface to each of these discussions was... "We as parents cannot make decisions for you. You must be prepared to make your own decisions when faced with a choice." We would then talk about choices and consequences but would never ask for a decision. Frequently, Cristy and Glen would talk about situations they had seen in school which would normally lead to a discussion about how they would have handled it. In the end, our objective was to encourage our kids to think through difficult issues that would certainly confront them well before they were forced to make an on-the-spot decision under pressure from their friends and peers. Growing up is not easy because certain decisions can have lifetime consequences. One of a parent's most critical roles is to prepare their children to make these decisions. In retrospect, Sunday night family dinners were one of the most important things we ever did as parents to help prepare our children for life's challenges that lay ahead.

Several years later, I became the second youngest Colonel in the Air Force and my family was there to share that important moment with me. Now, at 63 years old, my military career is but a memory, but after 41 years of marriage, my wife and I are still best friends, adventure partners, lovers, and each other's therapist and alter-ego. Our daughter and our son along with their spouses are our best friends. We look forward to annual ski vacations at Lake Tahoe with our daughter and her family while my son and I regularly windsurf together in Aruba as my wife and daughter-in-law relish their time together on the beach.

Life is all about balance and there are consequences if you overvalue one aspect of your life at the expense of another. I had put my career first at the expense of my family and *"Cats in the Cradle"* was a turning point that put my life back into the right balance – a timeless lesson of life learned through a simple song heard one morning on the long drive to work.

"Everyone can see we're together
And we fly just like birds of a feather
All of the people around us they say
Can they be that close?
Just let me state for the record
We're giving love in a family dose

We are family
I got all my sisters with me
We are family"
*(Sister Sledge ~ We are Family)*


That's one of my life's experiences, now what's yours?

# *Timeless Lessons*
## on
## Raising a Family

I'm gonna' watch you shine
Gonna' watch you grow
Gonna' paint a sign
So you'll always know
As long as one and one is two
There could never be a father
Who loved his daughter more than I love you
*(Paul Simon ~ Father & Daughter)*


~


When I see him smile
It fills me up with gladness
He's sunshine and he's laughter all combined
He picks me up, he cheers me through the bad times
A wondrous thing, my son and I
*(Neil Sedaka ~ My Son and I)*


~


I can tell you all I know, the where to go, the what to do
You can try to run but you can't hide
from what's inside of you
*(Steely Dan ~ Any Major Dude Will Tell You)*

Close your eyes
Have no fear
The monster's gone
He's on the run and your daddy's here
*(John Lennon ~ Beautiful Boy)*

~

Oh very young
What will you leave us this time
You're only dancing on this earth for a short while
*(Cat Stevens ~ Oh Very Young)*

~

What can you do when your dreams come true
And it's not quite like you planned?
*(The Eagles ~ After The Thrill Is Gone)*

~

Now honey, I don't wanna clip your wings
But a time comes when two people
should think of these things
Having a home and a family
Facing up to their responsibilities
*(Bruce Springsteen ~ I Wanna' Marry You)*

~

He'd say, I'm gonna' be like you Dad
I know I'm gonna' be like you
*(Harry Chapin ~ Cat's In The Cradle)*

Don't be a drop-out
Stay in school
Now listen to me kids
Without an education
Might as well be dead
*(James Brown ~ Don't Be a Dropout)*

~

Everyone's a winner
*(Hot Chocolate ~ Everyone's a Winner)*

~

First thing I remember was askin' papa, "Why?"
For there were many things I didn't know
And Daddy always smiled, took me by the hand
Sayin', "Someday you'll understand"

Well, I'm here to tell you now each and ev'ry mother's son
You better learn it fast, you better learn it young
'Cause, "someday" never comes
*(Creedence Clearwater Revival ~ Someday Never Comes)*

~

A child is born with a heart of gold
The way of the world makes his heart grow cold
*(Earth, Wind & Fire ~ That's The Way of The World)*

~

The ink is black, the page is white
Together we learn to read and write
A child is black, a child is white
Together they grow to see the light, to see the light
*(Three Dog Night ~ Black and White)*

So what do we do with our lives
We leave only a mark
Will our story shine like a light
Or end in the dark
Give it all or nothing
*(Tina Turner ~ We Don't Need Another Hero)*

~

Someone's going to have to explain it to me
I'm not sure what it means
My baby's feeling funny in the morning
She's having trouble getting into her jeans

Her waist-line seems to be expanding
Although she never feels like eating a thing
I guess well reach some understanding
When we see what the future will bring
*(Jackson Browne ~ Ready or Not)*

~

We're a winner
And never let anybody say
Boy, you can't make it
'Cause a feeble mind is in your way

No more tears do we cry
And we have finally dried our eyes
And we're movin' on up
*(The Impressions ~ Be a Winner)*

And when you finally fly away
I'll be hoping that I served you well
For all the wisdom of a lifetime
No one can ever tell
But whatever road you choose
I'm right behind you, win or lose
*(Rod Stewart ~ Forever Young)*

~

Good things might come to those who wait
But not to those who wait too late
*(Grover Washington, Jr & Bill Withers ~ Just The Two Of Us)*

~

Large hands lift him through the air
Excited eyes contain him there
The eyes of those he loves and knows
His puzzled head tipped to one side
Amazement swims in those bright green eyes

And all you ever learned from them
Until you grew much older
Did not compare with when they said,
"This is your brand new brother"
*(Elton John ~ The Greatest Discovery)*

~

Don't cross the river if you can't swim the tide
*(America ~ Don't Cross The River)*

People say, "believe half of what you see, son
And none of what you hear"
*(Marvin Gaye ~ I Heard It Through The Grapevine)*

~

(Father)
It's not time to make a change
Just relax, take it easy
You're still young, that's not your fault
There's so much you have to know

Take your time, think a lot
Think of everything you've got
For you will still be here tomorrow
But your dreams may not
*(Cat Stevens ~ Father and Son*

~

You hold the key to love and fear
All in your trembling hand
Just one key unlocks them both
It's there at your command
*(The Youngbloods ~ Let's Get Together)*

~

Is this the little boy I know
Playing with his Legos long ago
Watching all his programs on his TV screen
It can't be that far back as it might seem
*(Neil Sedaka ~ My Son and I)*

Who gets a second chance?
Who gets to have some fun?
Who gets to learn to dance?
Before his race is run
*(James Taylor ~ Mean Old Man)*

~

Mama told me when I was young
"Come sit beside me, my only son
And listen closely to what I say
And if you do this it will help you some sunny day"

"Forget your lust for the rich man's gold
All that you need is in your soul
And you can do this if you try
All that I want for you, my son, is to be satisfied"
*(Lynyrd Skynyrd ~ Simple Man)*

~

And as she blew the candles out
She turned five
How was I to know
It was the best thing
To come along for a long time
*(Carly Simon ~ The Best Thing)*

~

If you smile at me, I will understand
'Cause that is something everybody, everywhere does
In the same language
*(Crosby, Stills, Nash & Young ~ Wooden Ships)*

I am a child, I'll last a while
You can't conceive of the pleasure in my smile
You hold my hand, rough up my hair
It's lots of fun to have you there

You are a man, you understand
You pick me up and you lay me down again
You make the rules, you say what's fair
It's lots of fun to have you there
*(Neil Young ~ I'm a Child)*

~

A mother's child
A father's son
In this crowd, I'm only one
To tell you of your worth
As you spend your time on earth
*(Steve Miller Band ~ Seasons)*

~

There are some who will learn what teachers can teach
And those who believe what preachers may preach
One may demand, while others beseech
But just put out your hand and dare to reach
*(Edgar Winter ~ Keys To the Kingdom)*

~

I know nobody knows
Where it comes and where it goes
I know it's everybody's sin
You got to lose to know how to win
*(Aerosmith ~ Dream On)*

Did you ever see the faces of the children
They get so excited
Waking up on Christmas morning
Hours before the winter sun's ignited
They believe in dreams and all they mean
Including heaven's generosity
Peeping 'round the door
To see what parcels are for free
In curiosity
*(The Who ~ Christmas)*

~

Days turn into minutes, and minutes to memories
Life sweeps away the dreams that we have planned
You are young and you are the future
So suck it up and tough it out and be the best you can
*(John Mellencamp ~ Minutes to Memories)*

~

Come mothers and fathers
Throughout the land
And don't criticize
What you can't understand
Your sons and your daughters
Are beyond your command
*(Bob Dylan ~ The Times They Are a Changin')*

~

Here's what we call our golden rule
Have faith in you and the things you do
*(Sister Sledge ~ We Are Family)*

Mama'd come to school
And as I'd sit there softly crying
Teacher'd say, he's just not trying
He's got a good head if he'd apply it
But you know yourself
It's always somewhere else
*(Neil Diamond ~ Brooklyn Roads)*

~

You got to learn how to fall
Before you learn to fly
You got to drift in the breeze
Before you set your sails
*(Paul Simon ~ Learn How To Fall)*

~

Even when you're close to a dream
It can still let you down
You'll always have a chance to give up
So why do it now?
*(The Doobie Brothers ~ One By One)*

~

Look, he's crawling up my wall
Black and hairy, very small
Now he's up above my head
Hanging by a little thread

Now he's dropped on to the floor
Heading for the bedroom door
Maybe he's as scared as me
Where's he gone now, I can't see
*(The Who ~ Boris The Spider)*

And all they say is, "you ain't half the man he used to be
He had strength and he worked his life
to feed his family"
So if that's the way it has to be, I'll say goodbye to you
I'm not the guy, or so it seems, to fill my old man's shoes
*(Elton John ~ Into The Old Man's Shoes)*

~

When I was just a lad of ten, my father said to me
Come here and learn a lesson from the lovely lemon tree
Don't put your faith in love, my boy, my father said to me
I fear you'll find that love is like the lovely lemon tree

Lemon tree very pretty and the lemon flower is sweet
But the fruit of the poor lemon is impossible to eat
*(Peter, Paul & Mary ~ Lemon Tree)*

~

Some are bound for happiness, some are bound to glory
Some are bound to live with less, who can tell your story
*(Neil Young ~ See the Sky About To Rain)*

~

When you wish upon a star
Dreams will take you very far,
When you wish upon a dream
Life ain't always what it seems,

Once you see your light so clear
In the sky so very dear
You're a shining star, no matter who you are
Shining bright to see what you can truly be
*(Earth, Wind and Fire ~ Shining Star)*

100

Make someone happy
Make someone smile
Let's all work together
And make life worthwhile

Because together we'll stand
Divided we'll fall
Come on now people
Let's get on the ball
And work together
*(Canned Heat ~ Let's Work Together)*

Bruce
Springsteen

John
Mellencamp

Stevie
Nicks

PRPhotos.com

# Chapter 4

# Living Life

"I wouldn't change a thing
if I could live it all again"
*(Rod Stewart ~ If I Could Ever Change a Thing)*

# Introduction

We all remember certain times or events in our lives when we hear a certain song. Often, the music brings back memories as vivid as if they happened just yesterday. This is a story about vivid memories of living life in the late 80's. As Jimmy Buffett says...

"Some of its magic, some of its tragic
But I had a good life all the way"
*(Jimmy Buffett ~ He Went to Paris)*

In the summer of 1987, the Air Force sent us to Honolulu, Hawaii. Maybe it was compensation for the years spent in Turkey 15 years earlier. The ever-present sight of crystal clear waters, refreshing trade winds, the smell of the flowers on the trees, and the sound of the surf rolling onto the beach makes Hawaii a truly magical place to live. As we arrived, Cristy, our 17-year old daughter, was about to enter her first year of college and our son Glen was entering his sophomore year of high school. We had moved eight times in the past 20 years so it all seemed quite normal. We would soon find out that this move was anything but normal.

Cristy had earned a scholarship to the University of Michigan to study Aerospace Engineering. Because we had only been in Hawaii for a matter of weeks, we decided to let her travel to Ann Arbor, Michigan by herself and have my wife's sister (who lived nearby) get Cristy moved into the dormitory. Late one beautiful Hawaiian afternoon, we kissed Cristy goodbye and watched her board a United 747, with her favorite oversized, fluffy stuffed bear in hand, for the 10-hour flight to Chicago then on to Ann Arbor via Detroit. Our hearts sank as the 747 pushed back from the gate. At that moment, we knew that not going back with Cristy to help her get settled into her freshman year of college was possibly the biggest mistake of our lives. Two days later, we received a call reassuring us that she was settled into the dormitory and that all was well. Cristy seemed excited and not at all bothered by the fact that she was 8,000 miles from home. We were almost "empty nesters" but it didn't feel right.

"If I could turn the page in time
Then I'd rearrange just a day or two"
*(Fleetwood Mac ~ Little Lies)*

In 1987, Hawaii was ranked 45th out of the 50 states for its public school system so we set out to find a private school for Glen. Glen was a good student and an excellent soccer player which helped him get accepted to Punahou School, the same school President Obama graduated from eight years earlier. At the time, we didn't know much about the school but soon found out that Punahou was one of the top five private schools in the nation and had won the Hawaii state soccer championship the past five years. We were all elated until the first tuition bill arrived and Glen took his first round of mid-term exams. Punahou's academic credentials are impressive for a reason. The school sets extremely high standards and then expects their students to exceed them. Glen was faced with the greatest challenge of his young life. Fortunately, with months of very hard work on his part, the help and understanding of his teachers, and an excellent tutor, Glen was able to meet the school's high academic standards by the end of his first year. Three years later, he graduated and was awarded a full scholarship to the University of Michigan.

"Future's lookin' good at last
Rough times are all in the past
Oh and it's shinin' brightly
And I think it's gonna last"
*(Bob Seger ~ Shinin' Brightly)*

Cristy joined a sorority to expand her circle of friends and escape from a roommate from hell. But the great distance, very expensive long distance calls, and the absence of anything resembling email made it difficult to stay connected with her. Fortunately, I was required to return to Washington, DC several times a year so during the fall of her first semester I spent a few days visiting her at the University. Even though she had been gone only a few months, the moment I saw her, I knew she had changed. She was no longer Daddy's "little girl." Cristy had become a young woman, poised and self confident beyond her years. We quickly toured her dorm room and then she proudly showed me the campus and her sorority house. We had dinners together, hit several of the local hang-outs and talked about life and the future. It was a special time for Cristy and I and one that would be repeated a number of times in the months and years to come. These brief father - daughter visits created a bond between the two of us based on love, respect, and trust that will never be broken.

Cristy loves music as much as I do, so when she came home for Christmas that year, we went together and bought her the most expensive compact sound system we could find. It had detachable speakers an am/fm radio, and a dual cassette player. It was the mother of all stereo systems that could still fit into a college dorm room or a room in a sorority house. Armed with new stereo that everyone would be envious of and a handful of the latest Billy Joel cassettes, Cristy left Hawaii after Christmas to face her first Michigan winter and her roommate from hell!

"You know you got to go through hell
Before you get to heaven"
*(Steve Miller Band ~ Jet Airliner)*

Hawaii was the epicenter of the new sport of windsurfing which was suddenly receiving widespread media attention. Like any athletically talented 16-year old, Glen was drawn to this new and exciting "extreme sport." With his academics finally under control, Glen attacked the sport determined to master it within days instead of years. As it turned out, he had a talent for windsurfing and was soon entering competitions at Diamond Head against athletes twice his age. One Saturday as we sat on the beach at Diamond Head waiting for the wind to kick-in, Glen challenged me to learn the sport and offered to be my personal coach. I made every excuse I could think of but Glen would not take no for an answer. The next weekend, this 40-year old dad was in the water being taught a very unnatural sport from his 16-year old son. Son teaching father was certainly a role reversal but to this day, it created a bond between father and son like no other.

"Days, precious days... roll in and out like waves..."
*(Jimmy Buffett ~ Boats to Build)*

Once Glen became immersed in windsurfing, all of his free time was taken up with studying, soccer practice, or windsurfing. For all practical purposes, my wife and I found ourselves as "empty nesters" living in Hawaii. What a concept!

We made some great friends in Hawaii. All of us were essentially the same age and at the same stages in our lives. Our kids were exploring life on their own terms and didn't need or want help or advice from mom and dad. During several backyard conversations over Mai Tai's, we came to realize that we all shared a passion for the music we grew up with. As type-A Boomers, we took matters into our own hands and with split-second military precision, we found a nightspot on Waikiki that had a dance floor and a DJ that had an unbelievable library of classic rock tunes. Friday nights on Waikiki soon became a ritual. While our kids were out on dates on Friday or Saturday nights, we were having even more fun dancing to the music that we danced to 20 years earlier. The DJ was great... the more we danced, the more he would play. His music ran the gamut from The Stones ("Satisfaction" was a favorite) and the Beatles' "Hey Jude" to a healthy mix of Motown including the Temptations' "My Girl," Aretha Franklin's "Respect" and Wilson Picket's "Midnight Hour". Many nights we got home after our kids who would ask us the next morning where we

had been. The standard answer was... "Don't ask, don't tell."
The bond between the four couples grew as the months went
by and now, 20 years later, we still keep up with each other's
lives and the lives of our grown, married children. Nights
spent on Waikiki with special friends are cherished memories
that have led to lifetime friendships.

"I don't know
But I've been told
If you keep on dancing
You'll never grow old"
*(Steve Miller Band ~ Dance, Dance, Dance)*

Mothers have unbelievable patience. It must be something
in the "mother gene" that lets a mother and wife sit for hours
on a hot, windy beach with no toilets, no water, no shade,
and no place to sit except on an ice chest waiting for her son
and husband while they windsurfed together. Sitting was
frequently a family affair while we impatiently waited for the
wind to kick-in. It was about that time in Glen's life that he
was getting into music. One of his favorite groups was Styx
and *"Come Sail Away"* soon became his favorite song because
it spoke directly to what he was experiencing. My wife and I
remember sitting on the beach, watching the waves roll in at
Diamond Head listening to the song on our son's Walkman. To
this day, *"Come Sail Away"* not only takes our son back to a
very special place and time in his life, but it also takes his mom
and dad back to that beach at Diamond Head sharing time with
their son. Glen has long since married and he is living his
dream as an Air Force F-22 fighter pilot. Our mutual love for
the beach, warm tropical waters and windsurfing frequently

takes us to Aruba, one of the world's premier windsurfing locations. Glen continues to be my coach and windsurfing mentor and while the years have passed, our time spent in Hawaii 20 years ago forged a special bond that transcends time and age.


"I'm sailing away
Set an open course for the virgin sea
I've got to be free
Free to face the life that's ahead of me"
*(Styx ~ Come Sail Away)*


Cristy left home and never looked back, graduating from the University of Michigan in 1992 earning a Master's Degree in Aerospace Engineering. We later apologized to her for not taking her to college – a painful decision at the time and a mistake that we will always regret. Cristy shared with us how she coped with the initial loneliness by immersing herself in her studies, making friends in her sorority, and meeting a young man who would later become her husband. She also told us how music and the stereo system we bought during her freshman year helped get her through the time between visits back to Hawaii. Cristy married in August 1992. The day before her wedding, she gave the family a handwritten letter and a cassette tape which included 23 songs that held very special meaning to her. Her letter explained the significance of each song and the memories that they represented. Here are a few excerpts from her letter...

- ***Hollywood Nights*** by Bob Seger: "Dad... I'll never forget one summer in Hawaii. We were all at the Hard Rock Café for dinner and we were playing our little game of "who can name the song and artist the quickest wins..." Hollywood Nights by Bob Seger was playing and yes, you named it before me. Then the next day, when we were out shopping, you surprised me and bought the new Bob Seger Hollywood Nights cassette for me (I think you bought it just to rub it in that you had won the night before!)"

- ***Pretty Woman*** by Roy Orbison: "Mom... This is from the movie "Pretty Woman" which is an awesome movie. I've lost count how many times the two of us have watched it together. It is always such fun watching it with you. Not to mention that the scene where she is shopping on Rodeo Drive while this song is playing in the background reminds me of all the fun we have shopping together."

- ***Come Sail Away*** by Styx: "Glen... you used to always tell me how you felt like you were escaping from the world when you were out windsurfing. Whenever I was down, you would play this song. It seems to be your way of dealing with life's little problems and now I use the song to help me deal with little problems. It always makes me smile when I get frustrated because I think to myself... Where's Glen right now and I wonder what he's doing?"

- *Honolulu City Lights* by Keola & Kapono Beamer: "Mom, Dad and Glen... This song needs no explanation. Leaving the family for college was a living hell for me! This song reminds me of all the support you gave me during my first year in college. It also reminds me of all the incredible times we had together as a family in Hawaii."

- *American Pie* by Don McLean: "Mom, Dad, Glen, Tippy, Dusty (and all the other pets we've had). This song most reminds me of our entire family. Just because we truly are an "American Pie" family! Most people I know would kill to have a family like ours. It is something I'm very proud of!

As I was writing this book, I found Cristy's letter and called her. I asked her if she could still recall what was so special about those songs. In every case, she immediately repeated the story that she had written to us over 16 years ago almost word for word.

Try to tell me that music doesn't impact our lives in ways that we seldom realize or understand.

"Our memories of yesterday will last a lifetime
We'll take the best, forget the rest
And someday we'll find these are the best of times
These are the best of times"
*(Styx ~ The Best of Times)*


That's one of my life's experiences, now what's yours?

# Timeless Lessons
## on
## Living Life

Lord, this country's changed so fast
The future is the present
The present is in the past
*(Paul Simon ~ God Bless The Absentee)*

~

Life is very short and there's no time
For fussing and fighting my friend
*(The Beatles ~ We Can Work It Out)*

~

Never give up, never slow down
Never grow old, never ever die young
*(James Taylor ~ Never Die Young)*

~

But things in this life change very slowly
If they ever change at all
*(The Eagles ~ Sad Café)*

~

Life today is frittered away
You've got to simplify
Each in our own way, we live for today
*(America ~ Simple Life)*

And as I play the game of life
I try to make it better each and every day
*(John Lennon ~ Intuition)*

~

The line it is drawn
The curse it is cast
The slow one now
Will later be fast
As the present now
Will later be past
*(Bob Dylan ~ The Times They Are a Changin')*

~

Is it hard to make arrangements with yourself
When your old enough to repay but young enough to sell
*(Neil Young ~ Tell Me Why)*

~

Some hang on to what used to be
Live their lives looking behind
All we have is here and now
All our life out there to find
*(Joe Cocker and Jennifer Warnes ~ Up Where We Belong)*

~

Lucky I'm sane after all I've been through
I can't complain but sometimes I still do
Life's been good to me so far
*(The Eagles ~ Life's Been Good)*

I've been livin' for the moment
But I just can't have my way
And I'm afraid to go to sleep
'Cause tomorrow is today

I don't care to know the hour
'Cause it's passing anyway
I don't have to see tomorrow
'Cause I saw it yesterday
*(Billy Joel ~ Tomorrow is Today)*

~

I just want to celebrate another day of livin'
I just want to celebrate another day of life
*(Rare Earth ~ I Just Want to Celebrate)*

~

I do what I gotta' do
And I follow the rules
I didn't have an education
So I had to go back to school
*(James Brown ~ Don't Be a Dropout)*

~

No good deed goes unpunished
Nothing goes as planned
*(Jimmy Buffett ~ Just An Old Truth Teller)*

~

But there never seems to be enough time
To do the things you want to do
*(Jim Croce ~ Time In A Bottle)*

People come and go
Living other lives
Running everywhere at such a speed
Never taking time
To open up their eyes
Never knowing where life leads
*(Crosby, Stills, Nash & Young ~ Heartland)*

~

You can't always get what you want
But if you try sometime you just might find
You get what you need
*(The Rolling Stones ~ You Can't Always Get What You Want)*

~

I work my back 'till its racked with pain
The boss can't even recall my name
I feel like just another
Spoke in a great big wheel
Like a tiny blade of grass
In a great big field
*(Bob Seger ~ Feel Like a Number)*

~

And so it seems our destiny
To search and never rest
To ride that ever-changing wave
That never seems to crest
*(Bob Seger ~ No Man's Land)*

Well my instincts are fine
I had to learn to use them in order to survive
And time after time confirmed an old suspicion
It's good to be alive
*(John Lennon ~ Intuition)*

~

Sittin' in the morning sun
I'll be sittin' when the evening comes
Watching the ships roll in
Then I watch them roll away again
I'm sittin' on the dock of the bay
Watching the tide roll away
I'm just sittin' on the dock of the bay
Wasting time
*(Otis Redding ~ Dock of The Bay)*

~

Don't stop thinking about tomorrow
Don't stop, it'll soon be here
It'll be better than before
Yesterdays gone, yesterdays gone
*(Fleetwood Mac ~ Don't Stop)*

~

Like a river that don't know where it's flowing
I took a wrong turn and I just kept going
*(Bruce Springsteen ~ Hungry Heart)*

~

Living is easy with eyes closed
Misunderstanding all you see
*(The Beatles ~ Strawberry Fields Forever)*

And you'll find out every trick in the book
That there's only one way to get things done
You'll find out the only way to the top
Is looking out for number one
*(Bachman-Turner Overdrive ~ Looking Out For Number One)*

~

And time goes by so slowly
And time can do so much
*(Righteous Brothers ~ Unchained Melody)*

~

We've been spending too much of our lives
Living in a pastime paradise
Let's start living our lives
Living for the future paradise
*(Stevie Wonder ~ Pastime Paradise)*

~

Advice is cheap, you can take it from me
It's yours to keep 'cause opinions are free
*(Billy Joel ~ The Great Wall of China)*

~

I pressed my face to the window
I ran my fingers through my hair
I watched my life go around in a circle
And I realized that nobody but me cares
*(John Mellencamp ~ Kid Inside)*

We'd rather die on our feet
Than be livin' on our knees
*(James Brown ~ Say It Loud – I'm Black and I'm Proud)*

~

Like the fool I am and I'll always be
I've got a dream, I've got a dream
They can change their minds but they can't change me
*(Jim Croce ~ I Got A Name)*

~

All over the country I've seen it the same
Nobody's winnin' at this kind of game
We gotta' do better, it's time to begin
You know all the answers must come from within
*(Edgar Winter ~ Free Ride)*

~

If you've ever been taken for money
If you've ever gone down with your pride
If you've ever stood up for a good friend and lost
You know that the river is wide
*(Linda Ronstadt ~ Don't Cry Now)*

~

I was born a travelin' man
That's all I'll ever be
Movin' around from town to town
Is what makes me so free
*(Lynyrd Skynyrd ~ Travelin' Man)*

What a pity
That the people from the city
Can't relate to the slower things
That the country brings
*(Neil Young ~ Here We Are In The Years)*

~

Pulled my back and wrecked my car
Girlfriend stole my VCR
Letter came from Sixty Minutes
Say they wanna put me in it
Tell me my career just died
Years ago I might've cried
Now I'm just too old to do it
May be true, but screw it anyway

Me, I'm gonna' have a good day today
And I'm gonna' have a good time anyway
Put it all behind me, lay it all away
Gonna' be a good day today
*(Neil Diamond ~ Optimist Blues)*

~

You know the nearer your destination
The more you're slip slidin' away
*(Paul Simon ~ Slip Slidin' Away)*

~

Every morning when I wake,
a feeling soon begins to overtake me
Ringing in my ears resounds through my brain,
it finally surrounds me
There is fire, there is life, there is passion, fever and fury
There is love and there is hate,
there is longing, anger and worry
*(Eric Clapton ~ The Core)*

Well I was born in a small town
And I live in a small town
Probly' die in a small town

No, I cannot forget where it is that I come from
I cannot forget the people who love me
Yeah, I can be myself here in this small town
And people let me be just what I want to be
*(John Mellencamp ~ Small Town)*

~

Once I lived the life of a millionaire
Spending my money
Oh I didn't care
Taking my friends out
For a mighty good time
Oh we'd drink that good gin
Champagne and wine

But just as soon
As my money got low
I couldn't find nobody
And I had no place to go
*(Rod Stewart ~ Nobody Wants You When You're Down and Out)*

~

My hands were steady
My eyes were clear and bright
My walk had purpose
My steps were quick and light
And I held firmly
To what I felt was right
*(Bob Seger ~ Like a Rock)*

They paved paradise and put up a parking lot
With a pink hotel, a boutique and a swinging hot spot
Don't it always seem to go
That you don't know what you've got 'till it's gone
They paved paradise and put up a parking lot
*(Joni Mitchell ~ Big Yellow Taxi)*

~

Where and why I'm destined to go
Right here and now that's all I know
On either side future or past
Neither is real, both fade so fast
*(The Doobie Brothers ~ One by One)*

~

Early in the morning factory whistle blows
Man rises from bed and puts on his clothes
Man takes his lunch, walks out in the morning light
It's the working, the working, just the working life
*(Bruce Springsteen ~ Factory)*

~

And I won't break and I won't bend
And with the last breath we ever take
We're gonna get back to the simple life again
*(Elton John ~ Simple Life)*

~

To face the problems that everyone's found
We must replace what we took out of the ground
*(Grand Funk Railroad ~ Loneliness)*

# Introduction

*"Sunrise doesn't last all morning*
*A cloudburst doesn't last all day"*
*(The Beatles ~ All Things Must Pass)*

Three years into my married life, my wife and I were comfortably settled in San Antonio, Texas. We were enjoying our 18-month old daughter and doing what any newly married couple did living on a $284-a-month Air Force Lieutenant's salary! The memory of a Thursday afternoon in May 1971 is as vivid today as it was then when the Colonel called me into his office and told me that I was being reassigned to Turkey and I had 60 days to get there! My response was... "Where the hell is Turkey?"

I left work and hurried home to tell my wife who was three months pregnant. With a shocked and bewildered look, she asked... "Turkey? Where is Turkey?" and then promptly burst into tears. We dragged out the well-worn Rand McNally World Atlas and soon discovered that we were going to what appeared to be the end of the earth. A few days later, I was even more surprised to learn that my family could join me only if and when I found "suitable housing". The Colonel strongly suggested that I go to Turkey without my family. Not an option! After a tearful goodbye and two full days on three different airlines and at least 5 connections, I found myself in Adana, Turkey on a sweltering hot and humid July afternoon. Not the big city like Istanbul or Izmir but Adana... the agricultural capital of Turkey... just 12 miles from the Syrian border.

It being just a few years after the 1967 Arab-Israeli Six Day War and with ongoing tensions between the Turks and the Greeks, Incirlik Air Force Base was, at best, sparse. The architecture was simple... steel, pre-fabricated buildings, quonset huts, trailers, and a few cinderblock buildings. It was hot and dry with little to do but work and work-out. Finding my family an acceptable place to live proved to be my biggest challenge but finally, after almost four months, I watched my very pregnant wife, my 2-year old daughter and our 3-year old Border Collie emerge from a Pan American 707 at 8 pm on a dark and cold night in what seemed to be the middle of nowhere. I don't think I had ever loved my wife and being married more than at that moment.

We settled in and coped with the challenges of living with unexpected water and electricity outages, running short of toilet paper, and eating a lot of canned tuna fish and peanut butter. A young Air Force flight surgeon doubled as the OB/GYN Doc for what few women were brave enough to live there but Susann never complained. A few months later in the dead of winter, she courageously walked onto an Air Force C-130 cargo aircraft and flew two hours to Ankara (Turkey's capital) were our son was born in a 50-year old apartment building that the Air Force had converted into a hospital. We were young, didn't know any better, and life was good.

### "Only the strong survive"
*(REO Speedwagon ~ Only The Strong Survive)*

The two years in Turkey flew by, but gave us some of our fondest memories of the early years building a life together. We learned to work as a team to overcome both adversity and inconveniences. There was only one television channel – Armed Forces Network – which was like watching BBC! So, we played games, we listened to music, and we regularly took the kids to a nearby Mediterranean beach just minutes from the base where we marveled at the crystal clear, azure-blue waters. Most importantly, we explored a new culture and its people, we spent time together doing simple things, and we talked (and listened!) because all we had was each other. We became best friends in Turkey and developed a mutual trust and confidence that has helped take our marriage into its 41$^{st}$ year.

In 1971, there was no internet, no satellite TV, and no cell phones and in Turkey, there were no phones, period! If you wanted to talk to someone back home, it was by letter or through a Western Union telegram. For the four months before my family joined me, I lived in a 300 sq ft. bachelor officer's apartment with metal furniture, tile floors, and a small kitchen the size of most bathrooms. I was lonely and felt isolated. Thankfully, I brought my record collection with me and began to transfer my old albums onto cassettes and was proud of my first "Best Of" cassette featuring my favorite songs. I spent hours and hours, night after night sitting on the floor of my small, empty room listening to the music and carefully selecting my favorite tunes. For the first time, I actually heard the music I had been listening to for all those years. It was then that I began to truly appreciate the artistry of singers and songwriters such as Carole King, Jim Croce and groups like The Beatles, Crosby, Stills, Nash & Young, The Who, and Three Dog Night.

For four very long months, I fought off loneliness by reading my wife's weekly letters, living on memories, and listening to my music. Music helped me cope with a very difficult time in my young married life and led to a life-long love affair with the music of the 60's and 70's.

"When the day is so long that I can't hold on
When I'm down and I think my hope is gone
That's when the music takes me
Closer to a brighter day

I can feel my soul explodin'
There's a good feelin'
Helpin' me to find my way"
*(Neil Sedaka ~ That's When the Music Takes Me)*

That's one of my life's experiences, now what's yours?

# Timeless Lessons
## on
## Coping With the Unexpected


I was searching all the time
For something that I never lost or left behind
*(Jim Croce ~ Age)*


~


Well I finally got around to admit that I was the problem
When I use to put the blame
on everybody's shoulders but mine
*(The Eagles ~ One Day At A Time)*


~


You know, I've heard about people like me
But I never made the connection
They walk one road to set them free
And find they've gone the wrong direction
*(Don McLean ~ Crossroads)*


~


Why not think about times to come
And not about the things that you've done?
*(Fleetwood Mac ~ Don't Stop)*


~


It's a brand new morning of a brand new day
It's a brand new chance to make it all work out some way
*(Bob Seger ~ Brand New Morning)*

And it seems to me you lived your life
Like a candle in the wind
Never knowing who to cling to
When the rain set in
*(Elton John ~ Candle in The Wind)*

~

I got worries by the ton, gettin' cancer's only one
Overtaxed and alimonied, tired of eatin' fried baloney
I got burdens on my shoulders,
dying young or growin' older
There's some brain cells I'm missin'
But despite it all, I'd like to say

I'm gonna' have a good day today
Gonna' have a good time anyway
Put it all behind me, lay it all away
Gonna' be a good day today
*(Neil Diamond ~ Optimist Blues)*

~

Oh, won't somebody tell me
Tell me where have all the good times gone
Say that you remember
all those good old Four Tops songs
Won't somebody tell me
Where have all the good times gone
*(Elton John ~ Where Have All The Good Times Gone)*

~

Now troubles are many
They're as deep as a well
I can swear there ain't no Heaven
But I pray there ain't no hell
*(Blood, Sweat and Tears ~ When I Die)*

I wish you peace when the cold winds blow
Warmed by the fire's glow
I wish you comfort in the lonely times
And arms to hold you when you ache inside

I wish you hope when things are going bad
Kind words when times are sad
I wish you shelter from the raging wind
Cooling waters at the fever's end
*(The Eagles ~ I Wish You Peace)*

~

And night has given away
To the promise of another day
*(James Taylor ~ Another Day)*

~

So brothers and sisters and friends, dig this
Quit your dreaming all night
Stop pitying yourself and
Get up and fight
*(James Brown ~ America's My Home)*

~

I looked at your face every day
But I never saw it 'till I went away
*(Orleans ~ Still The One)*

In sixty-nine I was twenty-one and I called the road my own
I don't know when that road turned into the road I'm on
*(Jackson Browne ~ Running on Empty)*

~

I can see clearly now the rain is gone
I can see all obstacles in my way
Gone are the dark clouds that had me blind
It's gonna be a bright, bright
Sunshiny day
*(Johnny Nash ~ I Can See Clearly Now)*

~

I was always hearin' music, always wanna' play me some
As a full-time friend or the way to ease the end
of a woman that swayed me some
Hearin' those tunes always had a way
of soothin' out my soul
When times got hard and work got slow
it was music that kept me whole
*(The Doobie Brothers ~ Texas Lullaby)*

~

All this bitchin' and moanin' and pitchin' a fit
Get over it!  Get over it!
*(The Eagles ~ Get Over It)*

~

Yes, there are two paths you can go by
But in the long run
There's still time to change the road you're on
*(Led Zeppelin ~ Stairway to Heaven)*

Get up, get back on your feet
You're the one they can't beat and you know it
Come on, let's see what you've got
Just take your best shot and don't blow it
*(Styx ~ Fooling Yourself)*

~

Now that the time has come to see yourself
You always look the other way
*(John Lennon ~ I Don't Wanna Face It)*

~

Little darling, I feel that ice is slowly melting
Little darling, it seems like years since it's been clear
Here comes the sun, here comes the sun
And I say it's all right
*(The Beatles ~ Here Comes The Sun)*

~

And when ya got money, ya got lots of friends
Crowdin' 'round your door
When the money's gone
And all your spendin' ends
They won't be 'round anymore
*(Blood, Sweat & Tears ~ God Bless The Child)*

~

Well one thing you must admit
And you know it's true
The final decision is still up to you
*(Undisputed Truth ~ You Make Your Own Heaven
and Hell Right Here on Earth)*

My life is changing
In so many ways
I don't know who
To trust anymore
*(Neil Young ~ A Man Needs A Maid)*

~

Take it with a grain of salt
And laugh at all the complexities
*(Jimmy Buffett ~ The Good Fight)*

~

Oh, sometimes skies are cloudy
And sometimes skies are blue
And sometimes they say that you eat the bear
But sometimes the bear eats you
And sometimes I feel like I should go
Far, far away and hide
'Cause I keep a waitin' for my ship to come in
And all that ever comes is the tide
*(Jim Croce ~ Hard Time Losin' Man)*

~

Well we're living here in Allentown
And they're closing all the factories down
Out in Bethlehem they're killing time
Filling out forms
Standing in line
*(Billy Joel ~ Allentown)*

There are people who have let the problems of today
Lead them to conclude that for them life is not the way
But every problem has an answer and if yours you cannot find
You should talk it over with Him
He'll give you peace of mind
When you feel your life's too hard
Just go have a talk with God
*(Stevie Wonder ~ Have a Talk With God)*


~


When you're down and out, and your soul is bare
Just turn around, you will find me there
I will take your hand, I will dry your tears
I will comfort you when your hope has disappeared
*(Carole King ~ You Will Find Me There)*


~


Some will win, some will lose
Some were born to sing the blues
Oh, the movie never ends
It goes on and on and on and on
Don't stop believin'
Hold on to that feelin'
*(Journey ~ Don't Stop Believin')*


~


I guess I thought you'd be here forever
Another illusion I chose to create
You don't know what ya' got until it's gone
And I found out just a little too late
*(Chicago ~ Hard Habit to Break)*

Down on me oh, down on me
I said it looks like everybody in this whole round world
They're down on me
*(Janis Joplin ~ Down on Me)*

~

If the thorn of a rose is the thorn in your side
Then you're better off dead if you haven't yet died
*(Elton John ~ Better of Dead)*

~

But he sure found out the hard way
That dreams don't always come true
So he pawned all his hopes and even sold his old car
For a one way ticket back to the life he once knew
*(Gladys Knight & The Pips ~ Midnight Train to Georgia)*

~

We both were growin' older and
Wiser with our years
That's when I came to understand
The course his heart still steered

He died about a month ago
While winter filled the air
And though I cried I was so proud
To have loved a man so rare
*(Jimmy Buffett ~ The Captain and The Kid)*

When no-one else can understand me
When everything I do is wrong
You give me hope and consolation
You give me strength to carry on
And you're always there to lend a hand
In everything I do
That's the wonder
The wonder of you
*(Elvis Presley ~ The Wonder of You)*

~

I don't need you to worry for me 'cause I'm alright
I don't want you to tell me it's time to come home
I don't care what you say anymore, this is my life
Go ahead with your own life and leave me alone
*(Billy Joel ~ My Life)*

~

You never close your eyes anymore when I kiss your lips
And there's no tenderness like before in your fingertips
You've lost that lovin' feeling
Oh, you've lost that lovin' feeling
*(Righteous Brothers ~ You've Lost That Lovin' Feeling)*

~

Chromosomes and genes spawn these fateful scenes
Evolution can be mean, there's no "dumb ass" vaccine
Blame your DNA, you're a victim of your fate
It's human nature to miscalculate
*(Jimmy Buffett ~ Permanent Reminder
of A Temporary Feeling)*

Now it seems to me, some fine things
Have been laid upon your table
But you only want the ones that you can't get
*(The Eagles ~ Desperado)*

~

I'm on your side when times get rough
And friends just can't be found
Like a bridge over troubled water
I will ease your mind
*(Paul Simon ~ Bridge Over Troubled Water)*

~

Anybody here seen my old friend Martin?
Can you tell me where he's gone?
He freed a lot of people
But it seems the good they die young
*(Dion ~ Abraham, Martin and John)*

~

When day has left the night behind
And shadows roll across my mind
I sometimes find myself alone out walkin' the street
And when I'm feelin down and blue
Then all I do is think of you
And all my foolish problems seem to fade away
*(The Doobie Brothers ~ South City Midnight Lady)*

And the years rolled slowly past
And I found myself alone
Surrounded by strangers I thought were my friends
*(Bob Seger ~ Against The Wind)*

~

Like a ship without a compass on a cold lonely sea
No beacon light of love to guide me through
I lost the only treasure that means anything to me
What now, what next, where to?
*(Elvis Presley ~ What Now, What Next, Where To)*

~

Grew up with great expectations
Heard the promise and I knew the plan
They say people get what they deserve
But Lord, sometimes it's much worse than that
Oh Lord, what did I do
To deserve these empty hands
*(John Mellencamp ~ Empty Hands)*

~

If you're driftin' on an empty ocean
with no wind to fill your sail
the future, your horizon
it's like searchin' for the Holy Grail
You feel there's no tomorrow
as you look into the water below
It's only your reflection
and you still ain't got no place to go
*(Deep Purple ~ Sail Away)*

# The Eagles

To view the entire photo album go to
**listentothemusiclyrics.com**

© Henry Diltz/Corbis

# Chapter 6

# Growing Wiser, Not Older

"I hope I die before I get old"
*(The Who ~ My Generation)*

# Introduction

"I look pretty young, but I'm just backdated"
*(The Who ~ Substitute)*

A music revolution began in September 1966 with the introduction of the first compact cassette in America. However, it was not until 1971 that the compact cassette became a viable (and much more compact and mobile) alternative to the 12-inch vinyl LP and 45-rpm record. In '71, a high fidelity cassette tape deck combining Dolby noise-reduction technology and chromium dioxide ($CrO_2$) tapes, together with the ability to record music onto a cassette revolutionized the way we listened to music. By the mid 70's, most of us had transferred our old LPs and 45- singles to cassettes and then unceremoniously sold our old Beatles and Rolling Stones albums at garage sales. For most, this was our first attempt to create a compilation tape combining our favorite rock classics onto a single cassette. I recall spending hours and hours carefully selecting just the right songs to record on my "Best Of" cassette. Just as I was ready to record the last song on what would become the perfect tape, I hit the record button late and missed the first 3 bars of the song and had to start all over again. Damn it... hate it when that happens!

In July 1979, Sony introduced the first Walkman portable cassette player, but again, it was not until 1984 when they unveiled their audio-quality, second generation Walkman that people took notice and made the Walkman the birthday or Christmas gift of choice for the next 4 to 5 years. No sooner were we contently sitting on a beach or around the pool listening to our favorite music on our Walkmans, than some rich dude would walk by with something called a Compact Disk/CD. The CD was unveiled by Philips in 1982 and Billy Joel's *52nd Street* was the first album to be released on CD. Because of the high cost of both the CD players and disks, CD's did not become widely accepted until the late 80's and was the format of choice through the 90's until Apple unveiled the iPod in October 2001, launching music's digital revolution.

"Are you reelin' in the years?
Stowin' away the time?"
*(Steely Dan ~ Reelin' In The Years)*

Today the iPod/MP3 player is what the transistor radio was in the 60's, what the cassette tape was in the 70's, the Walkman in the 80's, and what the CD was in the 90's. However, there is a critical difference. With the advent of MP3 players and digital music downloads, songs are now just a mouse-click and $0.99 away. How often have you regretted selling or throwing away those old LPs as you searched to find a song that was once your favorite? The challenge is even more daunting when searching for that great "one-hit wonder" or a song from one of many "garage bands" from the 60's and 70's. Today, if you search iTunes or Amazon.com you can find what you are looking for... even that long-lost song thrown out when you finally cleaned out the garage in 1983. Digital music, iPods, and MP3 players have brought music back into our everyday lives. From Sirius Satellite Radio and iPod docking stations in your car, classic rock channels on your satellite TV, to an iPod in your briefcase when you travel, all of your favorite music is now accessible, inexpensive, and portable. Those who grew up with the music of the 60's and 70's can easily find those lost songs (and memories), build several playlists to fit your mood, and take it all with you on vacation, on business trips, or play it on your audio system at home while cooking dinner. The music revolution that began in the 60's continues today and is yet another reason why the music of the 60's and 70's appeals to three generations... not just those of us who grew up with it.

Digital music and the iPod gave me the ability to rebuild my music library. The journey can be addicting. You hear a long-since-forgotten song on your drive home from work so you drop your briefcase at the door and run to the computer to download the song (before you forget it) and carefully place it into one of your many playlists. Whether or not your life is now more in balance than it was when you were raising a family or pursuing your career, you owe it to yourself to make it a priority to listen to your favorite music. It has only been in the past few years that I have taken the time to listen to the music I had been enjoying all these years and realize what I had been missing. One of my favorite Eagles songs is "Already Gone" and when I finally took the time to listen to the lyrics, I was struck by a number of thought-provoking messages hidden within the song...

"Just remember this, my girl,
when you look up in the sky
You can see the stars but still not see the light"
*(The Eagles ~ Already Gone)*

And that was the inspiration for this book. Curiously, as I explained my project to friends, most would tell me about a particular song they remember from growing up in the 60's or 70's and the special significance it had in their lives. Frequently,

149

they could quote something from the lyrics... a message that they had carried with them for most of their lives. It struck me that my experience is not unique. Music is a universal language that captures every human emotion and can evoke thoughts and feelings that words alone cannot express. While I have always had a passion for music, I didn't realize until recently how it has impacted my life and how it continues to energize, inspire, and lift my spirits.

"So often times it happens
that we live our lives in chains
And we never even know we have the key"
(The Eagles ~ Already Gone)

Music changes people's lives in unusual and unsuspected ways. Lackland Air Force Base in San Antonio, Texas is the home of the Defense Language Institute where the Department of Defense teaches English to soldiers, sailors, and airmen from allied foreign countries. In 1991, I volunteered to host one of these students. I was surprised to meet my new "amigo"... an Air Force Colonel from Poland who was the first student from one of the former Soviet controlled East European block countries to attend the year-long school. Colonel Marek Ciszewski was a young, enthusiastic Mig 21 Fighter Pilot whose mission just a few years prior was to fly, fight, and win against NATO and US fighter jets. Oh, how times had changed.

At our first meeting, I was surprised to learn that, except for a slight accent, my new comrade in arms from Poland spoke English almost as well as I did. Not only did he have an excellent command of our everyday language, he was equally fluent in American slang, acronyms, and an occasional, well placed "expletive deleted." He had an infectious smile and sense of humor that he used to his advantage. Our friendship grew as he learned about life in America and I learned of his life behind the Iron Curtain. I asked Marek if he had been sent to a Russian English-language school prior to coming to the United States. I was surprised when he told me that he had taught himself English by listening to lyrics and reading album covers from the music of the 60's and 70's... especially The Beatles.

## "Keeping my mind on a better life"
*(Styx ~ Blue Collar Man)*

Marek and I have continued our friendship over the years with the help of email and digital photographs. When I began to write this book, I asked him to tell me more about how music impacted his life. His response was captivating.

Dear Steve,

"Thank you very, very much for giving me insight into your ambitious and a very far from a dynamic stereotype of a military person work. Reading the samples brought me back to some touching memories from my soul "hard disc", especially from my youth. Let me share with you just some personal feelings.

Taking a look into the musical fascinations of your youth brings a very special smile to my face since it shows me a substantial difference in our experiences in this area. For you it was just an ambiance you lived in. This surrounded you like the air. The music you are writing about was everywhere, in the shopping mall, on the radio, movies, TV. For me to listen to "your" music meant penetrating "the wall". There was not much rock available to me in Poland but listening to Radio Free Europe (a radio station located in Munich, Germany, sponsored by the US Government, which was jammed by the Russians). Listening to it demanded some skill and a lot of patience but it emitted some rock music to attract young listeners from "the block". We, the youngsters, created a net of fans who were exchanging the rare records and tapes that were smuggled from the West.

As something that was very much limited and difficult to get, the music represented a special value to me. I desperately wanted to understand what the songs were all about. This motivated me greatly to pick up some English. Consequently, to me listening to the music was the primary way to get in touch with the language. This was a hard experience, but the knowledge I got was firm and long lasting. And when the wall finally came down, I was one of the few to undertake the challenge of studying in the States where I met Colonel Steve Richards and....."

Marek

> "Still I think about myself
> As a lucky old dreamer
> If you're askin' me to tell
> Is it worth what I paid?
> You gonna hear me say
> Hell Yeah!"
> *(Neil Diamond ~ Hell Yeah)*

Carefully read Marek's letter again and you will not only read the words but feel the profound impact music had on his life. For most of us, music is but a simple pleasure, diversion, or hobby. It's something that we take for granted. For Marek, music was his window to the world. It was something that gave him a glimpse of life beyond the Iron Curtain and the repressive, totalitarian life in a communist country. Marek and his friends bought their rock music on the black market or had a friend smuggle records and tapes in from Western Europe. They wanted to learn about life in a free and open society and it was that passion for freedom that eventually brought the Berlin Wall down in 1989. Only with the passage of time did I finally appreciate the true value of music and the effect it can have on each of us as we navigate or way through the challenges of everyday life.

Music has touched our lives in ways that we don't fully understand. Maybe not to the extent that it impacted Colonel Marek Ciszewski, but the digital music revolution has brought the music we grew up with to the forefront of everyday life. The music of the 60's and 70's was born out of turbulent times in America's history. It was music that inspired, music that had a message, music that was often a call to action, music that could make you happy and music that could make you melancholy. Today, that music pulls memories deep from within our souls and takes us back, if even for a brief moment, to a different place and time. With the benefit of crystal clear, 20/20 hindsight, really *listen* to the music that you have been enjoying all these years. Appreciate the artistry, stories, messages, wit, and wisdom of this unique group of singers and songwriters whose music remains as popular today as it was 30 to 40 years ago.


"Life is what happens to you
While you're busy making other plans"
*(John Lennon ~ Beautiful Boy)*


That's one of my life's experiences, now what's yours?

# Timeless Lessons
on
# Growing Wiser... Not Older

Ain't it funny how we all turned out
I guess we are the people our parents warned us about
*(Jimmy Buffett ~ We're The People Our Parents Warned us About)*

~

Time passes and you must move on
Half the distance takes you twice as long
*(The Eagles ~ After The Thrill Is Gone)*

~

Good times, bad times
You know I've had my share
*(Led Zeppelin ~ Good Times and Bad Times)*

~

Sometimes you win, sometimes you lose
And most times you choose between the two
*(Carole King ~ Sweet Seasons)*

~

If I could save time in a bottle
The first thing that I'd like to do
Is to save every day
'Till eternity passes away
Just to spend them with you
*(Jim Croce ~ Time In A Bottle)*

Nothin' lasts forever but the earth and sky
And all your money won't another minute buy
*(Kansas ~ Dust in the Wind)*

~

Your conscience is a flawless
Judge and jury
*(Undisputed Truth ~ You Make Your Own Heaven and Hell
Right Here on Earth)*

~

So the secret to this life
Is so very easy to learn
If you ever love another
Never ask for anything in return
*(Steve Miller Band ~ Nothing Lasts)*

~

May the good Lord be with you
Down every road you roam
And may sunshine and happiness
surround you when you're far from home
And may you grow to be proud
Dignified and true
And do unto others
As you'd have done to you
Be courageous and be brave
And in my heart you'll always stay
Forever Young, Forever Young
*(Rod Stewart ~ Forever Young)*

Some of it's magic, some of it's tragic
But I had a good life all the way
*(Jimmy Buffett ~ He Went To Paris)*

~

The book of life is brief
*(Don McLean ~ And I Love You So)*

~

Wish I didn't know now what I didn't know then
*(Undisputed Truth ~ You Make Your Own Heaven and Hell
Right Here on Earth)*

~

I miss the hungry years
The once upon a time
The lovely long ago
We didn't have a dime
*(Neil Sedaka ~ The Hungry Years)*

~

If you believe in forever
Then life is just a one night stand...
*(Righteous Brothers ~ Rock and Roll Heaven)*

~

It's a hotel at best
You're here as a guest
You ought'a' make yourself at home
While you're waiting for the rest
*(Jackson Browne ~ Looking Into You)*

I've lived long enough to have learned
The closer you get to the fire the more you get burned
*(Billy Joel ~ A Matter of Trust)*

~

Let those winds of time blow over my head
I'd rather die while I'm livin' than live while I'm dead
*(Jimmy Buffett ~ Growing Older But Not Up)*

~

Paradise, can it be all I heard it was?
I close my eyes and maybe I'm already there
*(Styx ~ Blue Collar Man)*

~

When you look through the years
And see what you could have been
Oh, what might have been
If you'd had more time
*(Supertramp ~ Take The Long Way Home)*

~

Can't spend what you ain't got
Can't lose what you never had
*(The Allman Brothers Band ~ Can't Loose What You Never Had)*

~

The morning sun when it's in your face really shows your age
But that don't worry me none
In my eyes you're everything
*(Rod Stewart ~ Maggie May)*

Grow old along with me
The best is yet to be
When our time has come
We will be as one
God bless our love

Grow old along with me
Two branches of one tree
Face the setting sun
When the day is done
*(John Lennon ~ Grow Old With Me)*

~

I know that the door shuts just before
You get to the dream you see
*(The Byrds – Everybody's Been Burned)*

~

No use wondering where the years have gone
Time waits for no one, we all have to go on
*(Carole King ~ High Out Of Time)*

~

Some seek knowledge who claim to be wise
And may attain wisdom in other men's eyes
But the mind is a prison with thought it's disguise
*(Edgar Winter ~ Keys To the Kingdom)*

~

To make a chain of fools
You need a matching pair
*(Elton John ~ Passengers*

When I get older losing my hair
Many years from now
Will you still be sending me a valentine
Birthday greetings, bottle of wine
If I'd been out 'till quarter to three
Would you lock the door
Will you still need me, will you still feed me
When I'm sixty-four
*(The Beatles ~ When I'm 64)*

~

Lookin' back on time that's gone
I realized I might have been wrong
*(Steve Miller Band ~ Sacrifice)*

~

Well I've long since retired, my son's moved away
I called him up just the other day
I said I'd like to see you if you don't mind
He said I'd love to Dad if I can find the time

And as he hung up the phone it occurred to me
He'd grown up just like, my boy was just like me
*(Harry Chapin ~ Cat's In The Cradle)*

~

No it isn't strange after changes upon changes
We are more or less the same
*(Paul Simon ~ The Boxer)*

You're still the one I want to talk to in bed
Still the one that turns my head
We're still having fun and you're still the one

You're still the one that makes me laugh
Still the one that's my better half
We're still having fun and you're still the one
*(Orleans ~ Still The One)*

~

You pray a little more as you grow older
You get religion as your hair turns gray
But you don't need to worry about hereafter
Just worry what you're going to do today
*(Jimmy Buffett ~ The Christian)*

~

The best things in life are free
*(Neil Sedaka ~ Good Time Man)*

~

Well, all those people, they think they got it made
But I wouldn't buy, sell, borrow, or trade
Anything I have to be like one of them
I'd rather start all over again
*(Neil Young ~ Motion Pictures)*

~

As time goes on
I realize
Just what you mean to me
*(Chicago ~ Color My World)*

I wish those days could come back once more
Why did those days ever have to go
I wish those days could come back once more
Why did those days ever have to go, cause I loved 'em so
*(Stevie Wonder ~ I Wish)*

~

Some people seem obsessed with the morning
Get up early just to watch the sun rise
Some people like it more when there's fire in the sky
Worship the sun when it's high
Some people have to have their sultry evenings
Cocktails in the blue, red, and the grey
But I like every minute of the day
*(The Who ~ Blue, Red, and Grey)*

~

I saw a shooting star go by
It blazed a path across the sky
But the beauty did not last, no,
Some things just happen all to fast
*(Orleans ~ Love Takes Time)*

~

There's no use in asking why
It just turned out that way
*(The Eagles ~ The Sad Café)*

There are places I'll remember
All my life though some have changed
Some forever not for better
Some have gone and some remain
All these places have their moments
With lovers and friends I still can recall
Some are dead and some are living
In my life I've loved them all
*(The Beatles ~ In My Life)*

~

Sometimes in our lives we all have pain
We all have sorrow
But if we are wise
We know that there's always tomorrow
*(Bill Withers ~ Lean on Me)*

~

I want to sit at home in my rockin' chair
I don't want to travel the world
As far as I'm concerned I've had my share
But time's more precious than gold
I don't wanna' see another airplane seat
Or another hotel room
The home life to me seems really neat
I just wanna unpack for good
*(Fleetwood Mac ~ Homeward Bound)*

Now you tell me if I'm wrong
America is still the best country
And that's without a doubt
*(James Brown ~ America's My Home)*

~

Oh yeah, life goes on
Long after the thrill of livin' is gone
*(John Mellencamp ~ Jack and Diane)*

~

Time itself is bought and sold
The spreading fear of growing old
Contains a thousand foolish games
That we play
*(Neil Young ~ Here We are In The Years)*

~

We were the wild ones
So sure those days would never end
Now they're only memories, my friend
*(Styx ~ Dear John)*

~

The more we learn the less we know
What you keep is what you can't let go
*(Jimmy Buffett – Don't Chu' Know)*

Every year is getting shorter,
never seem to find the time
Plans that either come to naught,
or half a page of scribbled lines
*(Pink Floyd ~ Time)*

~

Well, I'm not the kind to live in the past
The years run too short and the days too fast
The things you lean on
Are the things that don't last
*(Al Stewart ~ Time Passages)*

# The
# Eagles

# Epilogue

# A Note to All You Boomers...

Here's how to get the music
you lost 30 years ago
and what to do with it once you've got it

"In the field of opportunity
It's plowin' time again
There ain't no way of telling
Where these seeds will rise or when"
*(Neil Young ~ Field of Opportunity)*

# Epilogue

*"For all those who don't feel as old as they are and never will"*
*(Jimmy Buffett ~ Growing Older But Not Up)*

## Grab Your iPod

Grab your iPod, if you don't own one, go buy one! Using the songs and lyrics in this book as a starting point, pull together a playlist of your favorite songs of the 60's and 70's. Start with your *"Best-of-the-Best 60's and 70's Rock"* but depending on where your search takes you, you may decide on separate playlists for love songs, light rock/easy listening, or music that brings back special memories. Download those songs (yes... you only pay $0.99 for just the songs that you want and not an entire CD... check the reference guide for suggested websites), load your playlists on your iPod or MP3 player and see what you have been missing all these years.

If the thought of this intimidates you, just ask your grandchildren, who can teach you in less than 30 minutes. Trust me, it's easy and it will be fun for both of you. Once your music has been loaded on your computer, explore the advantages of buying a Sonos or similar system that allows you to wirelessly stream your rediscovered music from your computer to your media center. You are now ready to enjoy the sound that only good speakers and a powerful receiver can deliver. Just close your eyes and be taken back to that Temptations concert in 1968 or to The Purple Passion fraternity or sorority party in 1972.

For those of you who are more tech-savvy, burn a copy of your "Best Of the 60's and 70's" playlist (no disco please) and give it to your children and/or grandchildren as a special birthday gift. Then, together, listen to some of the songs and tell them why a particular song is on your playlist. Talk about what you were doing when you first heard a song, why a song brings back special memories, or explain how a song helped you get through a difficult time. Sharing your innermost feelings with your family through your favorite music will give them the opportunity to better understand your life during a time when they were too young to remember.

> "I've had to pay my price
> The things I did not know at first
> I learned by doin' twice"
> *(Billy Joel ~ The Entertainer)*

## Become a Mentor

Our parents were born during the Great Depression and endured one of the most desperate times in American history. They learned to do more with less, they saved what little money they had, and used every leftover in the kitchen for another meal. They fought and sacrificed for us in World War II and they experienced the rise of communism and the dawn of the atomic age. From these experiences, they became independent and self-reliant and they developed an uncommon work ethic, a "never again" outlook on life, a sense of purpose, a mental toughness, and most of all, a true sense of honesty and personal integrity. They passed on those core values to our generation with a commitment to prepare us to have a better, more successful life than they had.

The true value of this book is that it provides the perfect vehicle to pass down to our children and grandchildren what we learned as we lived our everyday lives... much of it the hard way. Thirty to forty years ago all we really cared about was passing the Chemistry mid-term, getting a date for the fraternity party, finding a job, or scraping together enough money to put gas in our VW Beetle. Now, with the benefit of our life experiences, the messages contained in this book take on a more profound and personal meaning than they did when we were growing up. Using these messages, we can give our children and their children insight on how to avoid making some of the mistakes we made and how to get the most out of life each and every day.

> "I can tell you all I know
> The where to go, the what to do
> And you can try to run but you can't hide
> From what's inside of you"
> *(Steely Dan ~ Any Major Dude Will Tell You)*

Learning is often best achieved through vivid mental images. We can relate the various messages in this book to our experiences and bring them to life with a personal story. It's our challenge to paint a picture through the words and experiences we use as we discuss these quotes with our families. Here's how to do it...

√ Present each family member with a journal that will become their book of quotes. Don't pass up the opportunity to write a personal inscription on the inside cover of the journal. Ask everyone to write down quotes or inspirational messages that you discuss as a family. Encourage them to find their own quotes as they come across them from time to time and then jot down a few thoughts to help remind them of how it personally relates to them.

√ When possible, bring your adult children and/or grandchildren together, sit around the dining room table, and simply talk about a message or quote you have chosen (from this book or another) that has particular significance to you.

√ Using a real life experience, explain what the quote means to you and how it might help them work through a problem or avoid making a mistake later in life.

√ When you can't meet together as a family, email a quote each Sunday (without fail) and challenge everyone to take a few minutes to analyze its meaning. Once you begin, it's surprising how quickly your family will start looking forward to their Sunday quote!

√ Remind your family to turn to their journal when they are having a tough day, are frustrated or uncertain about what to do, or they just need a little encouragement or inspiration. Suggest that they take a quiet minute to thumb through their journal until they find a passage that will put the problem in perspective and help them make the right decision for the right reasons.


"Nothing survives
But the way we live our lives"
*(Jackson Browne ~ Daddy's Tune)*

This is a perfect way to bring families closer together, to encourage open communications, to talk about issues both big and small, and to build greater mutual trust and respect. Take your life experiences, the good ones and the bad, and use what you have learned to help guide your children and their children through life as our parents did for us.

"Songs of life, songs of hope
Songs to keep your dreams afloat"
*(Jimmy Buffett ~ Boats to Build)*

# Appendix

## Suggested Playlists

- Love Songs
- Music with a message
- Light Rock
- Rock

Billboard's Top 20 Rock Singles – 1960 to 1980

Billboard's Top 20 Soul/R&B Singles – 1960 to 1980

Rock and Roll Hall of Fame

## Resources

## Index

# Love Songs

| | |
|---|---|
| **Something** | The Beatles |
| **In My Life** | The Beatles |
| **Fooled Around and Fell In Love** | Elvin Bishop |
| **If** | Bread |
| **Up Where We Belong** | Joe Cocker & Jennifer Warnes |
| **Time In a Bottle** | Jim Croce |
| **Annie's Song** | John Denver |
| **After the Lovin'** | Engelbert Humperdinck |
| **The First Time Ever I Saw His Face** | Roberta Flack |
| **Escape (The Pena Colada Song)** | Rupert Homes |
| **Your Song** | Elton John |
| **The Time of My Life** | Bill Medley & Jennifer Warnes |
| **You're Still The One** | Orleans |

| | |
|---|---|
| **Unchained Melody** | The Righteous Brothers |
| **Crusin'** | Smokey Robinson |
| **Once, Twice, Three Times a Lady** | Lionel Richie |
| **Laughter in the Rain** | Neil Sedaka |
| **Nobody Does It Better** | Carly Simon |
| **When a Man Loves a Woman** | Percy Sledge |
| **Afternoon Delight** | Starland Vocal Band |
| **Have I Told You Lately That I Love You** | Rod Stewart |
| **You're In My Heart** | Rod Stewart |
| **How Sweet it Is To Be Loved By You** | James Taylor |
| **My Girl** | The Temptations |
| **My Eyes Adored You** | Frankie Valli |
| **Just The Two of Us** | Grover Washington & Bill Withers |
| **I Was Made To Love Her** | Stevie Wonder |

# Songs with a Message

**The Captain and the Kid**    Jimmy Buffett

**Boats to Build**    Jimmy Buffett

**Oysters and Pearls**    Jimmy Buffett

**Daddy's Tune**    Jackson Browne

**Cat's In The Cradle**    Harry Chapin

**America The Beautiful**    Ray Charles

**Rocky Mountain High**    John Denver

**One Day at A Time**    The Eagles / Joe Walsh

**I Wish You Peace**    The Eagles

**Don't Stop**    Fleetwood Mac

**Candle in The Wind**    Elton John

**Pink Houses**    John Mellencamp

**I Can See Clearly Now**    Johnny Nash

| | |
|---|---|
| **My Son and I** | Neil Sedaka |
| **The Hungry Years** | Neil Sedaka |
| **Father & Daughter** | Paul Simon |
| **For What It's Worth** | Buffalo Springfield |
| **Forever Young** | Rod Steward |
| **Father and Son** | Cat Stevens |
| **Fooling Yourself** | Styx |
| **Isn't She Lovely** | Stevie Wonder |

# Light Rock

| | |
|---|---|
| **The Weight** | The Band |
| **California Girls** | The Beach Boys |
| **Hay Jude** | The Beatles |
| **I Get By With A Little Help From My Friends** | The Beatles |
| **Here Comes The Sun** | The Beatles |
| **Ride Captain Ride** | The Blues Image |
| **Doctor My Eyes** | Jackson Browne |
| **Tempted By The Fruit of Another** | Paul Carrack & Squeeze |
| **Southern Cross** | Crosby, Stills & Nash |
| **South City Midnight Lady** | The Doobie Brothers |
| **Hotel California** | The Eagles |
| **Sunset Grille** | The Eagles |
| **Rocket Man** | Elton John |

| | |
|---|---|
| **Brandy (You're a Fine Girl)** | Looking Glass |
| **Drift Away** | Dobie Grey |
| **Lights** | Journey |
| **Do You Believe In Magic** | The Lovin' Spoonful |
| **Amie** | Pure Prairie League |
| **Time For Me To Fly** | REO Speedwagon |
| **Dock of the Bay** | Otis Redding |
| **All Night Long** | Lionel Richie |
| **My Whole World Ended** | David Ruffin |
| **Night Moves** | Bob Seger |
| **One of a Kind Love Affair** | The Spinners |
| **Take The Long Way Home** | Supertramp |
| **Ain't Too Proud To Beg** | The Temptations |
| **Love Is Alive** | Gary Wright |

# Rock

| | |
|---|---|
| **Get Back** | The Beatles |
| **Ramblin' Man** | Allman Brothers Band |
| **Celebration** | Kool & The Gang |
| **Feeling Stronger Everyday** | Chicago |
| **Reelin' In the Years** | Steely Dan |
| **Listen to the Music** | The Doobie Brothers |
| **Light My Fire** | The Doors |
| **Already Gone** | The Eagles |
| **Feels Like The First Time** | Foreigner |
| **Respect** | Aretha Franklin |
| **All Right Now** | Free |
| **No Sugar Tonight** | The Guess Who |
| **I Go To Extremes** | Billy Joel |

| | |
|---|---|
| **Saturday Night's All Right(for Fighting)** | Elton John |
| **Can't You See** | The Marshall Tucker Band |
| **Paper in Fire** | John Mellencamp |
| **Jet Airliner** | Steve Miller Band |
| **In The Midnight Hour** | Wilson Picket |
| **American Band** | Grand Funk Railroad |
| **Hollywood Nights** | Bob Seger |
| **Sweet Home Alabama** | Lynyrd Skynyrd |
| **Mighty Love** | The Spinners |
| **Glory Days** | Bruce Springsteen |
| **Maggie May** | Rod Stewart |
| **Satisfaction** | Rolling Stones |
| **You Can't Always Get What You Want** | Rolling Stones |
| **Gimme Shelter** | Rolling Stones |
| **Come Sail Away** | Styx |

| | |
|---|---|
| **I Know I'm Loosing You** | The Temptations |
| **Celebrate** | Three Dog Night |
| **Proud Mary** | Tina Turner |
| **Free Ride** | Edgar Winter |
| **Signed, Sealed and Delivered** | Stevie Wonder |
| **Hold on Loosely** | .38 Special |

# Billboard Magazine's

# Top 20 Rock Singles of the Year – 1960 to 1980*

# TOP ROCK/POP SINGLES OF THE YEAR – 1960

| | | |
|---|---|---|
| 1 | THEME FROM "A SUMMER PLACE" | Percy Faith |
| 2 | HE'LL HAVE TO GO | Jim Reeves |
| 3 | CATHY'S CLOWN | Everly Brothers |
| 4 | RUNNING BEAR | Johnny Preston |
| 5 | TEEN ANGEL | Mark Dinning |
| 6 | IT'S NOW OR NEVER | Elvis Presley |
| 7 | HANDY MAN | Jimmy Jones |
| 8 | I'M SORRY | Brenda Lee |
| 9 | STUCK ON YOU | Elvis Presley |
| 10 | THE TWIST | Chubby Checker |
| 11 | EVERYBODY'S SOMEBODY'S FOOL | Connie Francis |
| 12 | WILD ONE | Bobby Rydell |
| 13 | GREENFIELDS | Brothers Four |
| 14 | WHAT IN THE WORLD'S COME OVER YOU | Jack Scott |
| 15 | EL PASO | Marty Robbins |
| 16 | ALLEY-OOP | Hollywood Argyles |
| 17 | MY HEART HAS A MIND OF ITS OWN | Connie Francis |
| 18 | SWEET NOTHIN'S | Brenda Lee |
| 19 | ITSY BITSY TEENIE WEENIE YELLOW POLKADOT BIKINI | Brian Hyland |
| 20 | ONLY THE LONELY | Roy Orbison |

# TOP ROCK/POP SINGLES OF THE YEAR – 1961

| | | |
|---|---|---|
| 1 | TOSSIN' AND TURNIN' | Bobby Lewis |
| 2 | I FALL TO PIECES | Patsy Cline |
| 3 | MICHAEL | Highwaymen |
| 4 | CRYIN' | Roy Orbison |
| 5 | RUNAWAY | Del Shannon |
| 6 | MY TRUE STORY | Jive Five |
| 7 | PONY TIME | Chubby Checker |
| 8 | WHEELS | String-A-Longs |
| 9 | RAINDROPS | Dee Clark |
| 10 | WOODEN HEART | Joe Dowell |
| 11 | CALCUTTA | Lawrence Welk |
| 12 | TAKE GOOD CARE OF MY BABY | Bobby Vee |
| 13 | RUNNING SCARED | Roy Orbison |
| 14 | DEDICATED TO THE ONE I LOVE | Shirelles |
| 15 | LAST NIGHT | Mar-Keys |
| 16 | WILL YOU LOVE ME TOMORROW | Shirelles |
| 17 | EXODUS | Ferrante & Teicher |
| 18 | WHERE THE BOYS ARE | Connie Francis |
| 19 | HIT THE ROAD JACK | Ray Charles |
| 20 | SAD MOVIES MAKE ME CRY | Sue Thompson |

# TOP ROCK/POP SINGLES OF THE YEAR – 1962

| 1  | STRANGER ON THE SHORE        | Mr. Acker Bilk     |
|----|------------------------------|--------------------|
| 2  | I CAN'T STOP LOVING YOU       | Ray Charles        |
| 3  | MASHED POTATO TIME           | Dee Dee            |
| 4  | ROSES ARE RED                | Bobby Vinton       |
| 5  | THE STRIPPER                 | David Rose         |
| 6  | JOHNNY ANGEL                 | Shelley Fabares    |
| 7  | LOCO-MOTION                  | Little Eva         |
| 8  | LET ME IN                    | Sensations         |
| 9  | THE TWIST                    | Chubby Checker     |
| 10 | SOLDIER BOY                  | Shirelles          |
| 11 | HEY! BABY                    | Bruce Channel      |
| 12 | THE WANDERER                 | Dion               |
| 13 | DUKE OF EARL                 | Gene Chandler      |
| 14 | PALISADES PARK               | Freddy Cannon      |
| 15 | BREAKING UP IS HARD TO DO     | Neil Sedaka        |
| 16 | WOLVERTON MOUNTAIN           | Claude King        |
| 17 | SLOW TWISTIN'                | Chubby Checker     |
| 18 | IT KEEPS RIGHT ON A-HURTIN'   | Johnny Tillotson   |
| 19 | THE ONE WHO REALLY LOVES YOU  | Mary Wells         |
| 20 | GOOD LUCK CHARM              | Elvis Presley      |

# TOP ROCK/POP SINGLES OF THE YEAR – 1963

| | | |
|---|---|---|
| 1 | SUGAR SHACK | Jimmy Gilmer & The Fireballs |
| 2 | SURFIN' USA | The Beach Boys |
| 3 | THE END OF THE WORLD | Skeeter Davis |
| 4 | RHYTHM OF THE RAIN | Cascades |
| 5 | HE'S SO FINE | Chiffons |
| 6 | BLUE VELVET | Bobby Vinton |
| 7 | HEY PAULA | Paul & Paula |
| 8 | FINGERTIPS II | Little Stevie Wonder |
| 9 | WASHINGTON SQUARE | Village Stompers |
| 10 | IT'S ALL RIGHT | Impressions |
| 11 | CAN'T GET USED TO LOSING YOU | Andy Williams |
| 12 | MY BOYFRIEND'S BACK | The Angels |
| 13 | SUKIYAKI | Kyu Sakamoto |
| 14 | SHE'S A FOOL | Lesley Gore |
| 15 | SO MUCH IN LOVE | Tymes |
| 16 | PUFF THE MAGIC DRAGON | Peter, Paul & Mary |
| 17 | BLOWIN' IN THE WIND | Peter, Paul & Mary |
| 18 | I'M LEAVING IT UP TO YOU | Dale & Grace |
| 19 | DEEP PURPLE | Nino Tempo & April Stevens |
| 20 | WIPE OUT | Surfaris |

# TOP ROCK/POP SINGLES OF THE YEAR – 1964

| | | |
|---|---|---|
| 1 | I WANT TO HOLD YOUR HAND | The Beatles |
| 2 | SHE LOVES YOU | The Beatles |
| 3 | HELLO, DOLLY! | Louis Armstrong |
| 4 | OH, PRETTY WOMAN | Roy Orbison |
| 5 | I GET AROUND | The Beach Boys |
| 6 | EVERYBODY LOVES SOMEBODY | Dean Martin |
| 7 | MY GUY | Mary Wells |
| 8 | WE'LL SING IN THE SUNSHINE | Gale Garnett |
| 9 | LAST KISS | J. Frank Wilson & The Cavaliers |
| 10 | WHERE DID OUR LOVE GO | The Supremes |
| 11 | PEOPLE | Barbara Streisand |
| 12 | JAVA | Al Hirt |
| 13 | A HARD DAY'S NIGHT | The Beatles |
| 14 | LOVE ME DO | The Beatles |
| 15 | DO WAH DIDDY DIDDY | The Beatles |
| 16 | PLEASE, PLEASE ME | The Beatles |
| 17 | DANCING IN THE STREET | Martha & The Vandellas |
| 18 | LITTLE CHILDREN | Billy J. Kramer & The Dakotas |
| 19 | LOVE ME WITH ALL YOUR HEART | Ray Charles Singers |
| 20 | UNDER THE BOARDWALK | Drifters |

# TOP ROCK/POP SINGLES OF THE YEAR – 1965

| 1 | WOOLY BULLY | Sam the Sham & The Pharaohs |
| 2 | I CAN'T HELP MYSELF | The Four Tops |
| 3 | SATISFACTION | The Rolling Stones |
| 4 | YOU WERE ON MY MIND | We Five |
| 5 | YOU'VE LOST THAT LOVIN' FEELIN | Righteous Brothers |
| 6 | DOWNTOWN | Petula Clark |
| 7 | HELP! | The Beatles |
| 8 | CAN'T YOU HEAR MY HEARTBEAT | Herman's Hermits |
| 9 | CRYING IN THE CHAPEL | Elvis Presley |
| 10 | MY GIRL | The Temptations |
| 11 | HELP ME, RHONDA | The Beach Boys |
| 12 | KING OF THE ROAD | Roger Miller |
| 13 | THE BIRDS AND THE BEES | Jewel Aikens |
| 14 | HOLD ME, THRILL ME, KISS ME | Mel Carter |
| 15 | SHOTGUN | Jr. Walker & The All Stars |
| 16 | I GOT YOU BABE | Sonny & Cher |
| 17 | THIS DIAMOND RING | Gary Lewis & The Playboys |
| 18 | THE "IN" CROWD | Ramsey Lewis Trio |
| 19 | MRS. BROWN YOU'VE GOT A LOVELY DAUGHTER | Herman's Hermits |
| 20 | STOP! IN THE NAME OF LOVE | The Supremes |

# TOP ROCK/POP SINGLES OF THE YEAR – 1966

| | | |
|---|---|---|
| 1 | THE BALLAD OF THE GREEN BERETS | S/Sgt. Barry Sadler |
| 2 | CHERISH | The Association |
| 3 | YOU'RE MY SOUL AND INSPIRATION | The Righteous Brothers |
| 4 | REACH OUT I'LL BE THERE | The Four Tops |
| 5 | 96 TEARS | ? & The Mysterians |
| 6 | LAST TRAIN TO CLARKSVILLE | The Monkees |
| 7 | MONDAY, MONDAY | The Mamas & The Papas |
| 8 | YOU CAN'T HURRY LOVE | The Supremes |
| 9 | POOR SIDE OF TOWN | Johnny Rivers |
| 10 | CALIFORNIA DREAMIN' | The Mamas & The Papas |
| 11 | SUMMER IN THE CITY | The Lovin' Spoonful |
| 12 | BORN FREE | Roger Williams |
| 13 | THESE BOOTS ARE MADE FOR WALKIN' | Nancy Sinatra |
| 14 | WHAT BECOMES OF THE BROKENHEARTED | Jimmy Ruffin |
| 15 | STRANGERS IN THE NIGHT | Frank Sinatra |
| 16 | WE CAN WORK IT OUT | The Beatles |
| 17 | GOOD LOVIN' | The Young Rascals |
| 18 | WINCHESTER CATHEDRAL | New Vaudeville Band |
| 19 | HANKY PANKY | Tommy James & The Shondells |
| 20 | WHEN A MAN LOVES A WOMAN | Percy Sledge |

# TOP ROCK/POP SINGLES OF THE YEAR – 1967

| 1 | TO SIR WITH LOVE | Lulu |
|---|---|---|
| 2 | THE LETTER | The Box Tops |
| 3 | ODE TO BILLIE JOE | Bobby Gentry |
| 4 | WINDY | The Association |
| 5 | I'M A BELIEVER | The Monkees |
| 6 | LIGHT MY FIRE | The Doors |
| 7 | SOMETHIN' STUPID | Nancy Sinatra & Frank Sinatra |
| 8 | HAPPY TOGETHER | The Turtles |
| 9 | GROOVIN' | The Young Rascals |
| 10 | CAN'T TAKE MY EYES OFF YOU | Frankie Valli |
| 11 | LITTLE BIT O' SOUL | Music Explosion |
| 12 | I THINK WE'RE ALONE NOW | Tommy James & The Shondells |
| 13 | RESPECT | Aretha Franklin |
| 14 | I WAS MADE TO LOVE HER | Stevie Wonder |
| 15 | COME BACK WHEN YOU GROW UP | Bobby Vee & The Strangers |
| 16 | KIND OF A DRAG | The Buckinghams |
| 17 | SWEET SOUL MUSIC | Arthur Conley |
| 18 | EXPRESSWAY TO YOUR HEART | Soul Survivors |
| 19 | SOUL MAN | Sam & Dave |
| 20 | NEVER MY LOVE | The Association |

# TOP ROCK/POP SINGLES OF THE YEAR – 1968

| | | |
|---|---|---|
| 1 | HEY JUDE | The Beatles |
| 2 | LOVE IS BLUE | Paul Mauriat |
| 3 | HONEY | Bobby Goldsboro |
| 4 | SITTIN' ON THE DOCK OF THE BAY | Otis Redding |
| 5 | PEOPLE GOT TO BE FREE | The Rascals |
| 6 | SUNSHINE OF YOUR LOVE | Cream |
| 7 | THIS GUY'S IN LOVE WITH YOU | Herb Alpert |
| 8 | THE GOOD, THE BAD AND THE UGLY | Hugo Montenegro |
| 9 | MRS. ROBINSON | Simon & Garfunkel |
| 10 | TIGHTEN UP | Archie Bell & The Drells |
| 11 | HARPER VALLEY PTA | Jeannie C. Riley |
| 12 | LITTLE GREEN APPLES | O. C. Smith |
| 13 | MONY, MONY | Tommy James & The Shondells |
| 14 | HELLO, I LOVE YOU | The Doors |
| 15 | YOUNG GIRL | Gary Puckett & The Union Gap |
| 16 | CRY LIKE A BABY | The Box Tops |
| 17 | STONED SOUL PICNIC | The Fifth Dimension |
| 18 | GRAZING IN THE GRASS | Hugh Masekela |
| 19 | MIDNIGHT CONFESSIONS | Grass Roots |
| 20 | DANCE TO THE MUSIC | Sly & The Family Stone |

# TOP ROCK/POP SINGLES OF THE YEAR – 1969

| | | |
|---|---|---|
| 1 | SUGAR, SUGAR | Archies |
| 2 | AQUARIUS/LET THE SUNSHINE IN | The Fifth Dimension |
| 3 | I CAN'T GET NEXT TO YOU | The Temptations |
| 4 | HONKY TONK WOMEN | The Rolling Stones |
| 5 | EVERYDAY PEOPLE | Sly & The Family Stone |
| 6 | DIZZY | Tommy Roe |
| 7 | HOT FUN IN THE SUMMERTIME | Sly & The Family Stone |
| 8 | I'LL NEVER FALL IN LOVE AGAIN | Tom Jones |
| 9 | BUILD ME UP BUTTERCUP | Foundations |
| 10 | CRIMSON AND CLOVER | Tommy James & The Shondells |
| 11 | ONE | Three Dog Night |
| 12 | CRYSTAL BLUE PERSUASION | Tommy James & The Shondells |
| 13 | HAIR | The Cowsills |
| 14 | TOO BUSY THINKING ABOUT MY BABY | Marvin Gaye |
| 15 | LOVE THEME FROM ROMEO AND JULIET | Henry Mancini |
| 16 | GET TOGETHER | The Youngbloods |
| 17 | GRAZIN' IN THE GRASS | Friends of Distinction |
| 18 | SUSPICIOUS MINDS | Elvis Presley |
| 19 | PROUD MARY | Creedence Clearwater Revival |
| 20 | WHAT DOES IT TAKE TO WIN YOUR LOVE | Jr. Walker & The All Stars |

# TOP ROCK/POP SINGLES OF THE YEAR – 1970

| 1 | BRIDGE OVER TROUBLED WATER | Simon & Garfunkel |
|---|---|---|
| 2 | CLOSE TO YOU | The Carpenters |
| 3 | AMERICAN WOMAN | The Guess Who |
| 4 | RAINDROPS KEEP FALLIN' ON MY HEAD | B.J. Thomas |
| 5 | WAR | Edwin Starr |
| 6 | AIN'T NO MOUNTAIN HIGH ENOUGH | Diana Ross |
| 7 | I'LL BE THERE | The Jackson 5 |
| 8 | GET READY | Rare Earth |
| 9 | LET IT BE | The Beatles |
| 10 | BAND OF GOLD | Freda Payne |
| 11 | MAMA TOLD ME NOT TO COME | Three Dog Night |
| 12 | EVERYTHING IS BEAUTIFUL | Ray Stevens |
| 13 | MAKE IT WITH YOU | Bread |
| 14 | HITCHIN' A RIDE | Vanity Fare |
| 15 | ABC | The Jackson 5 |
| 16 | THE LOVE YOU SAVE | The Jackson 5 |
| 17 | CRACKLIN' ROSIE | Neil Diamond |
| 18 | CANDIDA | Dawn |
| 19 | THANK YOU (FALLETTIN ME BE MICE ELF AGIN) | Sly & The Family Stone |
| 20 | SPILL THE WINE | Eric Burden & War |

# TOP ROCK/POP SINGLES OF THE YEAR – 1971

| 1 | JOY TO THE WORLD | Three Dog Night |
|---|---|---|
| 2 | MAGGIE MAY | Rod Stewart |
| 3 | I FEEL THE EARTH MOVE | Carole King |
| 4 | ONE BAD APPLE | Osmonds |
| 5 | HOW CAN YOU MEND A BROKEN HEART | The Bee Gees |
| 6 | INDIAN RESERVATION | The Raiders |
| 7 | GO AWAY LITTLE GIRL | Donny Osmond |
| 8 | TAKE ME HOME, COUNTRY ROADS | John Denver |
| 9 | JUST MY IMAGINATION | The Temptations |
| 10 | KNOCK THREE TIMES | Dawn |
| 11 | ME AND BOBBY MCGEE | Janis Joplin |
| 12 | TIRED OF BEING ALONE | Al Green |
| 13 | WANT ADS | Honey Cone |
| 14 | SMILING FACES SOMETIMES | Undisputed Truth |
| 15 | TREAT HER LIKE A LADY | Cornelius Brothers & Sister Rose |
| 16 | BROWN SUGAR | The Rolling Stones |
| 17 | YOU'VE GOT A FRIEND | James Taylor |
| 18 | MR. BIG STUFF | Jean Knight |
| 19 | DO YOU KNOW WHAT I MEAN | Lee Michaels |
| 20 | THE NIGHT THEY DROVE OLD DIXIE DOWN | Joan Baez |

# TOP ROCK/POP SINGLES OF THE YEAR – 1972

| | | |
|---|---|---|
| 1 | THE FIRST TIME EVER I SAW YOUR FACE | Roberta Flack |
| 2 | ALONE AGAIN NATURALLY | Gilbert O'Sullivan |
| 3 | AMERICAN PIE | Don McLean |
| 4 | WITHOUT YOU | Nilsson |
| 5 | CANDY MAN | Sammy Davis, Jr. |
| 6 | I GOTCHA' | Joe Tex |
| 7 | LEAN ON ME | Bill Withers |
| 8 | BABY DON'T GET HOOKED ON ME | Mac Davis |
| 9 | BRAND NEW KEY | Melanie |
| 10 | DADDY DON'T YOU WALK SO FAST | Wayne Newton |
| 11 | LET'S STAY TOGETHER | Al Green |
| 12 | BRANDY | Looking Glass |
| 13 | OH GIRL | Chi-Lites |
| 14 | NICE TO BE WITH YOU | Gallery |
| 15 | MY DING-A-LING | Chuck Berry |
| 16 | IF LOVING YOU IS WRONG, I DONT WANT TO BE RIGHT | Luther Ingram |
| 17 | HEART OF GOLD | Neil Young |
| 18 | BETCHA' BY GOLLY, WOW | Stylistics |
| 19 | I'LL TAKE YOU THERE | The Staple Singers |
| 20 | BEN | Michael Jackson |

# TOP ROCK/POP SINGLES OF THE YEAR – 1973

| | | |
|---|---|---|
| 1 | TIE A YELLOW RIBBON 'ROUND THE OLD OAK TREE | Tony Orlando & Dawn |
| 2 | BAD, BAD LEROY BROWN | Jim Croce |
| 3 | KILLING ME SOFTLY WITH HIS SONG | Roberta Flack |
| 4 | LET'S GET IT ON | Marvin Gaye |
| 5 | MY LOVE | Paul McCartney & Wings |
| 6 | WHY ME | Kris Kristofferson |
| 7 | CROCODILE ROCK | Elton John |
| 8 | WILL IT GO ROUND IN CIRCLES | Billy Preston |
| 9 | YOU'RE SO VAIN | Carly Simon |
| 10 | TOUCH ME IN THE MORNING | Diana Ross |
| 11 | THE NIGHT THE LIGHTS WENT OUT IN GEORGIA | Vicki Lawrence |
| 12 | PLAYGROUND IN MY MIND | Clint Holmes |
| 13 | BROTHER LOUIE | Stories |
| 14 | DELTA DAWN | Helen Reddy |
| 15 | ME AND MRS. JONES | Billy Paul |
| 16 | FRANKENSTEIN | The Edgar Winter Group |
| 17 | DRIFT AWAY | Dobie Gray |
| 18 | LITTLE WILLY | Sweet |
| 19 | YOU ARE THE SUNSHINE OF MY LIFE | Stevie Wonder |
| 20 | HALF BREED | Cher |

# TOP ROCK/POP SINGLES OF THE YEAR – 1974

| | | |
|---|---|---|
| 1 | THE WAY WE WERE | Barbara Streisand |
| 2 | SEASONS IN THE SUN | Terry Jacks |
| 3 | LOVE'S THEME | Love Unlimited Orchestra |
| 4 | COME AND GET YOUR LOVE | Redbone |
| 5 | DANCING MACHINE | The Jackson 5 |
| 6 | THE LOCO-MOTION | Grand Funk Railroad |
| 7 | TSOP | MFSB |
| 8 | THE STREAK | Ray Stevens |
| 9 | BENNIE AND THE JETS | Elton John |
| 10 | ONE HELL OF A WOMAN | Mac Davis |
| 11 | UNTIL YOU COME BACK TO ME | Aretha Franklin |
| 12 | JUNGLE BOOGIE | Kool & The Gang |
| 13 | MIDNIGHT AT THE OASIS | Maria Muldaur |
| 14 | YOU MAKE ME FEEL BRAND NEW | Stylistics |
| 15 | SHOW AND TELL | Al Wilson |
| 16 | SPIDERS AND SNAKES | Jim Stafford |
| 17 | ROCK ON | David Essex |
| 18 | SUNSHINE ON MY SHOULDER | John Denver |
| 19 | SIDESHOW | Blue Magic |
| 20 | HOOKED ON A FEELING | Blue Swede |

# TOP ROCK/POP SINGLES OF THE YEAR – 1975

| | | |
|---|---|---|
| 1 | LOVE WILL KEEP US TOGETHER | Captain & Tennille |
| 2 | RHINESTONE COWBOY | Glen Campbell |
| 3 | PHILADELPHIA FREEDOM | Elton John |
| 4 | BEFORE THE NEXT TEARDROP FALLS | Freddy Fender |
| 5 | MY EYES ADORED YOU | Frankie Valli |
| 6 | SHINING STAR | Earth, Wind & Fire |
| 7 | FAME | David Bowie |
| 8 | LAUGHTER IN THE RAIN | Neil Sedaka |
| 9 | ONE OF THESE NIGHTS | The Eagles |
| 10 | THANK GOD I'M A COUNTRY BOY | John Denver |
| 11 | JIVE TALKIN' | The Bee Gees |
| 12 | BEST OF MY LOVE | The Eagles |
| 13 | LOVIN' YOU | Minnie Riperton |
| 14 | KUNG FU FIGHTING | Carl Douglas |
| 15 | BLACK WATER | The Doobie Brothers |
| 16 | BALLROOM BLITZ | Sweet |
| 17 | HEY WON'T YOU PLAY ANOTHER SOMEBODY DONE SOMEBODY WRONG SONG | BJ Thomas |
| 18 | HE DON'T LOVE YOU LIKE I LOVE YOU | Tony Orlando & Dawn |
| 19 | AT SEVENTEEN | Janis Ian |
| 20 | PICK UP THE PIECES | Average White Band |

# TOP ROCK/POP SINGLES OF THE YEAR – 1976

| 1 | SILLY LOVE SONGS | Wings |
| 2 | DON'T GO BREAKING MY HEART | Elton John & Kiki Dee |
| 3 | DISCO LADY | Johnnie Taylor |
| 4 | OH, WHAT A NIGHT | The Four Seasons |
| 5 | PLAY THAT FUNKY MUSIC | Wild Cherry |
| 6 | KISS AND SAY GOODBYE | Manhattans |
| 7 | LOVE MACHINE | The Miracles |
| 8 | 50 WAYS TO LEAVE YOUR LOVER | Paul Simon |
| 9 | LOVE IS ALIVE | Gary Wright |
| 10 | A FIFTH OF BEETHOVEN | Walter Murphy & The Big Apple Band |
| 11 | SARA SMILE | Daryl Hall & John Dates |
| 12 | AFTERNOON DELIGHT | Starland Vocal Band |
| 13 | I WRITE THE SONGS | Barry Manilow |
| 14 | FLY, ROBIN, FLY | Silver Convention |
| 15 | LOVE HANGOVER | Diana Ross |
| 16 | GET CLOSER | Seals & Crofts |
| 17 | MORE, MORE, MORE | Andrea True Connection |
| 18 | BOHEMIAN RHAPSODY | Queen |
| 19 | MISTY BLUE | Dorothy Moore |
| 20 | BOOGIE FEVER | Sylvers |

# TOP ROCK/POP SINGLES OF THE YEAR – 1977

| | | |
|---|---|---|
| 1 | TONIGHT'S THE NIGHT | Rod Stewart |
| 2 | I JUST WANT TO BE YOUR EVERYTHING | Andy Gibb |
| 3 | BEST OF MY LOVE | The Emotions |
| 4 | LOVE THEME FROM "A STAR IS BORN" | Barbra Streisand |
| 5 | ANGEL IN YOUR ARMS | Hot |
| 6 | I LIKE DREAMIN' | Kenny Nolan |
| 7 | DON'T LEAVE ME THIS WAY | Thelma Houston |
| 8 | YOUR LOVE HAS LIFTED ME HIGHER AND HIGHER | Rita Coolidge |
| 9 | UNDERCOVER ANGEL | Alan O'Day |
| 10 | TORN BETWEEN TWO LOVERS | Mary MacGregor |
| 11 | I'M YOUR BOOGIE MAN | K.C. & The Sunshine Band |
| 12 | DANCING QUEEN | Abba |
| 13 | YOU MAKE ME FEEL LIKE DANCING | Leo Sayer |
| 14 | MARGARITAVILLE | Jimmy Buffett |
| 15 | TELEPHONE LINE | Electric Light Orchestra |
| 16 | WHAT'CHA GONNA DO? | Pablo Cruise |
| 17 | DO YOU WANNA' MAKE LOVE | Peter McCann |
| 18 | SIR DUKE | Stevie Wonder |
| 19 | HOTEL CALIFORNIA | The Eagles |
| 20 | GOT TO GIVE IT UP | Marvin Gaye |

# TOP ROCK/POP SINGLES OF THE YEAR – 1978

| 1 | SHADOW DANCING | Andy Gibb |
|---|---|---|
| 2 | NIGHT FEVER | The Bee Gees |
| 3 | YOU LIGHT UP MY LIFE | Debby Boone |
| 4 | STAYIN' ALIVE | The Bee Gees |
| 5 | KISS YOU ALL OVER | Exile |
| 6 | HOW DEEP IS YOUR LOVE | The Bee Gees |
| 7 | BABY COME BACK | Player |
| 8 | LOVE IS THICKER THAN WATER | Andy Gibb |
| 9 | BOOGIE OOGIE OOGIE | A Taste of Honey |
| 10 | THREE TIMES A LADY | The Commodores |
| 11 | GREASE | Frankie Valli |
| 12 | I GO CRAZY | Paul Davis |
| 13 | YOU'RE THE ONE THAT I WANT | John Travolta & Olivia Newton-John |
| 14 | EMOTION | Samantha Sang |
| 15 | LAY DOWN SALLY | Eric Clapton |
| 16 | MISS YOU | The Rolling Stones |
| 17 | JUST THE WAY YOU ARE | Billy Joel |
| 18 | WITH A LITTLE LUCK | Wings |
| 19 | IF I CAN'T HAVE YOU | Yvonne Elliman |
| 20 | DANCE, DANCE, DANCE | Chic |

# TOP ROCK/POP SINGLES OF THE YEAR – 1979

| | | |
|---|---|---|
| 1 | MY SHARONA | Knack |
| 2 | BAD GIRLS | Donna Summer |
| 3 | LE FREAK | Chic |
| 4 | DA YA THINK I'M SEXY | Rod Stewart |
| 5 | REUNITED | Peaches & Herb |
| 6 | I WILL SURVIVE | Gloria Gaynor |
| 7 | HOT STUFF | Donna Summer |
| 8 | Y.M.C.A. | Village People |
| 9 | RING MY BELL | Anita Ward |
| 10 | SAD EYES | Robert John |
| 11 | TOO MUCH HEAVEN | The Bee Gees |
| 12 | MACARTHUR PARK | Donna Summer |
| 13 | WHEN YOU'RE IN LOVE WITH A BEAUTIFUL WOMAN | Dr. Hook |
| 14 | MAKIN' IT | David Naughton |
| 15 | FIRE | The Pointer Sisters |
| 16 | TRAGEDY | The Bee Gees |
| 17 | A LITTLE MORE LOVE | Olivia Newton-John |
| 18 | HEART OF GLASS | Blondie |
| 19 | WHAT A FOOL BELIEVES | The Doobie Brothers |
| 20 | GOOD TIMES | Chic |

# TOP ROCK/POP SINGLES OF THE YEAR – 1980

| | | |
|---|---|---|
| 1 | CALL ME | Blondie |
| 2 | ANOTHER BRICK IN THE WALL | Pink Floyd |
| 3 | MAGIC | Olivia Newton-John |
| 4 | ROCK WITH YOU | Michael Jackson |
| 5 | DO THAT TO ME ONE MORE TIME | Captain & Tennille |
| 6 | CRAZY LITTLE THING CALLED LOVE | Queen |
| 7 | COMING UP | Paul McCartney |
| 8 | FUNKYTOWN | Lipps, Inc. |
| 9 | IT'S STILL ROCK AND ROLL TO ME | Billy Joel |
| 10 | THE ROSE | Bette Midler |
| 11 | ESCAPE (THE PINA COLADA SONG) | Rupert Holmes |
| 12 | CARS | Gary Human |
| 13 | CRUISIN' | Smokey Robinson |
| 14 | WORKING MY WAY BACK TO YOU | The Spinners |
| 15 | LOST IN LOVE | Air Supply |
| 16 | LITTLE JEANNIE | Elton John |
| 17 | RIDE LIKE THE WIND | Cristopher Cross |
| 18 | UPSIDE DOWN | Diana Ross |
| 19 | PLEASE DON'T GO | K.C. & The Sunshine Band |
| 20 | BABE | Styx |

# Billboard Magazine's

## Top 20 Soul Singles of the Year – 1960 to 1980*

*Reprinted by permission of Billboard Research Services

# TOP SOUL SINGLES OF THE YEAR – 1960

| | | |
|---|---|---|
| 1 | KIDDIO | Brook Benton |
| 2 | BABY | Brook Benton & Dinah Washington |
| 3 | FOOL IN LOVE | Ike & Tina Turner |
| 4 | THE TWIST | Chubby Checker |
| 5 | CHAIN GANG | Sam Cooke |
| 6 | MONEY | Barrett Strong |
| 7 | LET'S GO, LET'S GO, LET'S GO | Hank Ballard & the Midnighters |
| 8 | FINGER POPPIN' TIME | Hank Ballard & the Midnighters |
| 9 | A WOMAN, A LOVER, A FRIEND | Jackie Wilson |
| 10 | SAVE THE LAST DANCE FOR ME | Drifters |
| 11 | DOGGIN' AROUND | Jackie Wilson |
| 12 | GEORGIA ON MY MIND | Ray Charles |
| 13 | THIS BITTER EARTH | Dinah Washington |
| 14 | FANNIE MAE | Buster Brown |
| 15 | HE WILL BREAK YOUR HEART | Jerry Butler |
| 16 | A ROCKIN' GOOD WAY | Dinah Washington |
| 17 | MY DEAREST DARLING | Etta James |
| 18 | WHITE SILVER SANDS | Bill Black's Combo |
| 19 | THERE'S SOMETHING ON YOUR MIND | Bobby Marchan |
| 20 | ALL I COULD DO WAS CRY | Etta James |

# TOP SOUL SINGLES OF THE YEAR – 1961

| | | |
|---|---|---|
| 1 | TOSSIN' AND TURNIN' | Bobby Lewis |
| 2 | IT'S GONNA' WORK OUT FINE | Ike & Tina Turner |
| 3 | DON'T CRY NO MORE | Bobby Bland |
| 4 | HIDEAWAY | Freddy King |
| 5 | SHOP AROUND | The Miracles |
| 6 | MY TRUE STORY | Jive Five |
| 7 | I LIKE IT LIKE THAT | Chris Kenner |
| 8 | STAND BY ME | Ben E King |
| 9 | MOTHER-IN-LAW | Ernie K-Doe |
| 10 | ALL IN MY MIND | Maxine Brown |
| 11 | I PITY THE FOOL | Bobby Bland |
| 12 | EVERY BEAT OF MY HEART | The Pips |
| 13 | BABY, YOU'RE RIGHT | James Brown |
| 14 | LAST NIGHT | The Mar-Keys |
| 15 | FOR MY BABY | Brook Benton |
| 16 | BOLL WEEVIL SONG | Brook Benton |
| 17 | HIT THE ROAD JACK | Ray Charles |
| 18 | I DON'T MIND | James Brown |
| 19 | YA-YA | Lee Dorsey |
| 20 | WILL YOU LOVE ME TOMORROW | Shirelles |

# TOP SOUL SINGLES OF THE YEAR – 1962

| | | |
|---|---|---|
| 1 | SOUL TWIST | King Curtis |
| 2 | I CAN'T STOP LOVING YOU | Ray Charles |
| 3 | TWIST AND SHOUT | Isley Brothers |
| 4 | BRING IT ON HOME TO ME | Sam Cooke |
| 5 | LOST SOMEONE | James Brown & The Famous Flames |
| 6 | MASHED POTATO TIME | Dee Dee Sharp |
| 7 | ANY DAY NOW | Chuck Jackson |
| 8 | SNAP YOUR FINGERS | Joe Henderson |
| 9 | PARTY LIGHTS | Claudine Clark |
| 10 | YOU'LL LOSE A GOOD THING | Barbara Lynn |
| 11 | THE DUKE OF EARL | Gene Chandler |
| 12 | TWISTIN' THE NIGHT AWAY | Sam Cooke |
| 13 | SOMETHING'S GOT A HOLD ON ME | Etta James |
| 14 | I KNOW | Barbara George |
| 15 | SOLDIER BOY | The Shirelles |
| 16 | I NEED YOUR LOVIN' | Don Gardner & Dee Dee Ford |
| 17 | NIGHT TRAIN | James Brown & The Famous Flames |
| 18 | THE ONE WHO REALLY LOVES YOU | Mary Wells |
| 19 | THE TWIST | Chubby Checker |
| 20 | DON'T PLAY THAT SONG | Ben E King |

# TOP SOUL SINGLES OF THE YEAR – 1963

| 1 | PART TIME LOVE | Little Johnny Taylor |
| 2 | MOCKINGBIRD | Inez Foxx |
| 3 | BABY WORKOUT | Jackie Wilson |
| 4 | FINGERTIPS (Part II) | Little Stevie Wonder |
| 5 | HEAT WAVE | Martha & The Vandellas |
| 6 | PRIDE AND JOY | Marvin Gaye |
| 7 | THE LOVE OF MY MAN | Theola Gilgore |
| 8 | CRY BABY | Garnett Minims & The Enchanters |
| 9 | YOU'VE REALLY GOT A HOLD ON ME | The Miracles |
| 10 | HELLO STRANGER | Barbara Lewis |
| 11 | JUST ONE LOOK | Doris Troy |
| 12 | THE MONKEY TIME | Major Lance |
| 13 | THAT'S THE WAY LOVE IS | Bobby Bland |
| 14 | OUR DAY WILL COME | Ruby & The Romantics |
| 15 | HE'S SO FINE | Chiffons |
| 16 | IF YOU WANNA BE HAPPY | Jimmy Soul |
| 17 | TWO LOVERS | Mary Wells |
| 18 | EASIER SAID THAN DONE | Essex |
| 19 | MICKEY'S MONKEY | The Miracles |
| 20 | WALK LIKE A MAN | The Four Seasons |

# TOP SOUL SINGLES OF THE YEAR – 1964

There were no Soul Singles charts published by Billboard during 1964

# TOP SOUL SINGLES OF THE YEAR – 1965

| | | |
|---|---|---|
| 1 | I CAN'T HELP MYSELF | The Four Tops |
| 2 | IN THE MIDNIGHT HOUR | Wilson Pickett |
| 3 | SHOTGUN | Jr Walker & the All Stars |
| 4 | I DO LOVE YOU | Billy Stewart |
| 5 | YES, I'M READY | Barbara Mason |
| 6 | PAPA'S GOT A BRAND NEW BAG | James Brown |
| 7 | THE TRACK OF MY TEARS | The Miracles |
| 8 | WE'RE GONNA MAKE IT | Little Milton |
| 9 | TONIGHT'S THE NIGHT | Solomon Burke |
| 10 | I'LL BE DOGGONE | Marvin Gaye |
| 11 | NOTHING CAN STOP ME | Gene Chandler |
| 12 | DON'T MESS UP A GOOD THING | Fontella Bass & Bobby McClure |
| 13 | MY GIRL | The Temptations |
| 14 | STOP IN THE NAME OF LOVE | The Supremes |
| 15 | OO WEE BABY I LOVE YOU | Fred Hughes |
| 16 | NOWHERE TO RUN | Martha & The Vandellas |
| 17 | SINCE I LOST MY BABY | The Temptations |
| 18 | IT'S A MAN DOWN THERE | G L Crockett |
| 19 | OO BABY, BABY | The Miracles |
| 20 | BABY I'M YOURS | Barbara Lewis |

# TOP SOUL SINGLES OF THE YEAR – 1966

| | | |
|---|---|---|
| 1 | HOLD ON! I'M COMIN' | Sam & Dave |
| 2 | COOL JERK | Capitols |
| 3 | BABY SCRATCH MY BACK | Slim Harpo |
| 4 | AIN'T TOO PROUD TO BEG | The Temptations |
| 5 | BAREFOOTIN' | Robert Parker |
| 6 | 634-5789 | Wilson Pickett |
| 7 | UP TIGHT | Stevie Wonder |
| 8 | WHEN A MAN LOVES A WOMAN | Percy Sledge |
| 9 | WHAT BECOMES OF THE BROKENHEARTED | Jimmy Ruffin |
| 10 | BEAUTY IS ONLY SKIN DEEP | The Temptations |
| 11 | LOVE MAKES THE WORLD GO ROUND | Deon Jackson |
| 12 | KNOCK ON WOOD | Eddie Floyd |
| 13 | LOVE IS A HURTIN' THING | Lou Rawls |
| 14 | OPEN THE DOOR TO YOUR HEART | Darrell Banks |
| 15 | DON'T MESS WITH BILL | Marvelettes |
| 16 | I LOVE YOU 1000 TIMES | The Platters |
| 17 | SUNNY | Bobby Hebb |
| 18 | WADE IN THE WATER | Ramsey Lewis |
| 19 | ROAD RUNNER | Jr Walker & the All Stars |
| 20 | GOING TO A GO-GO | The Miracles |

# TOP SOUL SINGLES OF THE YEAR – 1967

| | | |
|---|---|---|
| 1 | RESPECT | Aretha Franklin |
| 2 | SOUL MAN | Sam & Dave |
| 3 | I NEVER LOVED A MAN THE WAY I LOVE YOU | Aretha Franklin |
| 4 | MAKE ME YOURS | Bettye Swann |
| 5 | I WAS MADE TO LOVE HER | Stevie Wonder |
| 6 | COLD SWEAT | James Brown |
| 7 | ARE YOU LONELY FOR ME | Freddie Scott |
| 8 | TELL IT LIKE IT IS | Aaron Neville |
| 9 | SWEET SOUL MUSIC | Arthur Conley |
| 10 | YOUR LOVE KEEPS LIFTING ME HIGHER AND HIGHER | Jackie Wilson |
| 11 | MERCY, MERCY, MERCY | Cannonball Adderley |
| 12 | BABY I LOVE YOU | Aretha Franklin |
| 13 | JIMMY MACK | Martha & The Vandellas |
| 14 | SOUL FINGER | Bar-Kays |
| 15 | GET ON UP | Esquires |
| 16 | THE HUNTER GETS CAPTURED BY THE GAME | Marvelettes |
| 17 | LOVE IS HERE AND NOW YOU'RE GONE | Diana Ross & The Supremes |
| 18 | STAND BY ME | Spyder Turner |
| 19 | HIP-HUG-HER | Booker T & The MG's |
| 20 | EXPRESSWAY TO YOUR HEART | Soul Survivors |

# TOP SOUL SINGLES OF THE YEAR – 1968

| | | |
|---|---|---|
| 1 | SAY IT LOUD I'M BLACK AND I'M PROUD | James Brown |
| 2 | SLIP AWAY | Clarence Carter |
| 3 | SITTIN' ON THE DOCK OF THE BAY | Otis Redding |
| 4 | GRAZING IN THE GRASS | Hugh Masekela |
| 5 | YOU'RE ALL I NEED TO GET BY | Marvin Gaye & Tammi Terrell |
| 6 | STAY IN MY CORNER | The Dells |
| 7 | WE'RE A WINNER | The Impressions |
| 8 | I WISH IT WOULD RAIN | The Temptations |
| 9 | TIGHTEN UP | Archie Bell & The Drells |
| 10 | LOVER'S HOLIDAY | Peggy Scott & JoJo Benson |
| 11 | SINCE YOU'VE BEEN GONE | Aretha Franklin |
| 12 | THINK | Aretha Franklin |
| 13 | CHAIN OF FOOLS | Aretha Franklin |
| 14 | COWBOYS TO GIRLS | The Intruders |
| 15 | DANCE TO THE MUSIC | Sly & The Family Stone |
| 16 | NEVER GIVE YOU UP | Jerry Butler |
| 17 | THE HORSE | Cliff Nobles & Co |
| 18 | GIRL WATCHER | O'Kaysions |
| 19 | LOVE MAKES A WOMAN | Barbara Acklin |
| 20 | LA LA MEANS I LOVE YOU | Delfonics |

# TOP SOUL SINGLES OF THE YEAR – 1969

| 1 | WHAT DOES IT TAKE TO WIN YOUR LOVE | Jr Walker & the All Stars |
| 2 | I CAN'T GET NEXT TO YOU | The Temptations |
| 3 | MOTHER POPCORN (Part I) | James Brown |
| 4 | TOO BUSY THINKING ABOUT MY BABY | Marvin Gaye |
| 5 | IT'S YOUR THING | Isley Brothers |
| 6 | ONLY THE STRONG SURVIVE | Jerry Butler |
| 7 | CHOKIN' KIND | Joe Simon |
| 8 | HOT FUN IN THE SUMMERTIME | Sly & The Family Stone |
| 9 | JEALOUS KIND OF FELLOW | Garland Green |
| 10 | GRAZING IN THE GRASS | Friends of Distinction |
| 11 | SHARE YOUR LOVE WITH ME | Aretha Franklin |
| 12 | RUNAWAY CHILD, RUNNING WILD | The Temptations |
| 13 | CHOICE OF COLORS | The Impressions |
| 14 | THAT'S THE WAY LOVE IS | Marvin Gaye |
| 15 | YOUR GOOD THING | Lou Rawls |
| 16 | OH, WHAT A NIGHT | The Dells |
| 17 | CAN I CHANGE MY MIND | Tyrone Davis |
| 18 | EVERYDAY PEOPLE | Sly & The Family Stone |
| 19 | BABY, I'M FOR REAL | Originals |
| 20 | COLOR HIM FATHER | Winstons |

# TOP SOUL SINGLES OF THE YEAR – 1970

| | | |
|---|---|---|
| 1 | I'LL BE THERE | The Jackson 5 |
| 2 | LOVE ON A TWO WAY STREET | The Moments |
| 3 | SIGNED, SEALED, DELIVERED | Stevie Wonder |
| 4 | THE LOVE YOU SAVE | The Jackson 5 |
| 5 | THANK YOU (Falletin Me Be Mice Elf Agin) | Sly & the Family Stone |
| 6 | RAINY NIGHT IN GEORGIA | Brook Benton |
| 7 | BALL OF CONFUSION | The Temptations |
| 8 | TURN BACK THE HANDS OF TIME | Tyrone Davis |
| 9 | COLE, COOKE & REDDING/SUGAR SUGAR | Wilson Pickett |
| 10 | EXPRESS YOURSELF | Charles Wright & The Watts 103rd Street Rhythm Band |
| 11 | STEAL AWAY | Johnnie Taylor |
| 12 | PSYCHEDELIC SHACK | The Temptations |
| 13 | IT'S A SHAME | The Spinners |
| 14 | CALL ME | Aretha Franklin |
| 15 | PATCHES | Clarence Carter |
| 16 | DIDN'T I BLOW YOUR MIND THIS TIME | Delfonics |
| 17 | GROOVY SITUATION | Gene Chandler |
| 18 | ABC | The Jackson 5 |
| 19 | I WANT YOU BACK | The Jackson 5 |
| 20 | DON'T PLAY THAT SONG | Aretha Franklin |

# TOP SOUL SINGLES OF THE YEAR – 1971

| | | |
|---|---|---|
| 1 | MR BIG STUFF | Jean Knight |
| 2 | WHAT'S GOING ON | Marvin Gaye |
| 3 | WANT ADS | Honey Gone |
| 4 | TIRED OF BEING ALONE | Al Green |
| 5 | SPANISH HARLEM | Aretha Franklin |
| 6 | JUST MY IMAGINATION | The Temptations |
| 7 | BRIDGE OVER TROUBLED WATER | Aretha Franklin |
| 8 | THIN LINE BETWEEN LOVE AND HATE | The Persuaders |
| 9 | NEVER CAN SAY GOODBYE | The Jackson 5 |
| 10 | MAKE IT FUNKY (Part 1) | James Brown |
| 11 | GROOVE ME | King Floyd |
| 12 | TRAPPED BY A THING CALLED LOVE | Denise LaSalle |
| 13 | DON'T KNOCK MY LOVE | Wilson Pickett |
| 14 | STICK-UP | Honey Cone |
| 15 | PUSH & PULL (Part 1) | Rufus Thomas |
| 16 | MERCY, MERCY ME | Marvin Gaye |
| 17 | SMILING FACES SOMETIMES | Undisputed Truth |
| 18 | SHE'S NOT JUST ANOTHER WOMAN | 8th Day |
| 19 | WHAT'CHA SEE IS WHAT'CHA GET | Dramatics |
| 20 | THE LOVE WE HAD | The Dells |

# TOP SOUL SINGLES OF THE YEAR – 1972

| | | |
|---|---|---|
| 1 | LET'S STAY TOGETHER | Al Green |
| 2 | I'LL TAKE YOU THERE | The Staple Singers |
| 3 | IF LOVING YOU IS WRONG, I DON'T WANT TO BE RIGHT | Luther Ingram |
| 4 | IN THE RAIN | The Dramatics |
| 5 | OH GIRL | CM-Lites |
| 6 | BACK STABBERS | O'Jays |
| 7 | THAT'S THE WAY I FEEL ABOUT 'CHA | Bobby Womack |
| 8 | EVERYBODY PLAYS THE FOOL | Main Ingredient |
| 9 | DO THE FUNKY PENGUIN | Rufus Thomas |
| 10 | I GOT 'CHA | Joe Tex |
| 11 | YOU SAID A BAD WORD | Joe Tex |
| 12 | CLEAN UP WOMAN | Betty Wright |
| 13 | LEAN ON ME | Bill Withers |
| 14 | OUTA-SPACE | Billy Preston |
| 15 | GOODFOOT (PART 1) | James Brown |
| 16 | WOMAN'S GOTTA' HAVE IT | Bobby Womack |
| 17 | DAY DREAMING | Aretha Franklin |
| 18 | POWER OF LOVE | Joe Simon |
| 19 | LOOK WHAT YOU DONE FOR ME | Al Green |
| 20 | FREDDIE'S DEAD | Curtis Mayfield |

# TOP SOUL SINGLES OF THE YEAR – 1973

| | | |
|---|---|---|
| 1 | LET'S GET IT ON | Marvin Gaye |
| 2 | SUPERSTITION | Stevie Wonder |
| 3 | NEITHER ONE OF US WANTS TO BE THE FIRST TO SAY GOODBYE | Gladys Knight & the Pips |
| 4 | ME AND MRS JONES | Billy Paul |
| 5 | WHY CAN'T WE LIVE TOGETHER | Timmy Thomas |
| 6 | ONE OF A KIND LOVE AFFAIR | The Spinners |
| 7 | LOVE TRAIN | O'Jays |
| 8 | DOING IT TO DEATH | Fred Wesley & The JB's |
| 9 | MIDNIGHT TRAIN TO GEORGIA | Gladys Knight & The Pips |
| 10 | LOVE JONES | Brighter Side of Darkness |
| 11 | I'M GONNA' LOVE YOU JUST A LITTLE MORE | Berry White |
| 12 | COULD IT BE I'M FALLING IN LOVE | The Spinners |
| 13 | MASTERPIECE | The Temptations |
| 14 | NATURAL HIGH | Bloodstone |
| 15 | PILLOW TALK | Sylvia |
| 16 | THAT LADY | Isley Brothers |
| 17 | GIVE YOUR BABY A STANDING OVATION | The Dells |
| 18 | KEEP ON TRUCKIN' | Eddie Kendricks |
| 19 | IF YOU WANT ME TO STAY | Sly & The Family Stone |
| 20 | THE WORLD IS A GHETTO | War |

# TOP SOUL SINGLES OF THE YEAR – 1974

| | | |
|---|---|---|
| 1 | FEEL LIKE MAKING LOVE | Roberta Flack |
| 2 | BOOGIE DOWN | Eddie Kendricks |
| 3 | JUNGLE BOOGIE | Kool & the Gang |
| 4 | BEST THING THAT EVER HAPPENED TO ME | Gladys Knight & the Pips |
| 5 | LOOKING FOR LOVE | Bobby Womack |
| 6 | ROCK YOUR BABY | George McCrae |
| 7 | THE PAYBACK | James Brown |
| 8 | MIGHTY LOVE (Part 1) | The Spinners |
| 9 | DANCING MACHINE | The Jackson 5 |
| 10 | SEXY MAMA | Moments |
| 11 | PUT YOUR HANDS TOGETHER | O'Jays |
| 12 | ROCK THE BOAT | Hues Corporation |
| 13 | TSOP | MFSB |
| 14 | I'M IN LOVE | Aretha Franklin |
| 15 | CAN'T GET ENOUGH OF YOUR LOVE | Berry White |
| 16 | TRYING TO HOLD ON TO MY WOMAN | Lamont Dozier |
| 17 | OUTSIDE WOMAN | Bloodstone |
| 18 | BE THANKFUL FOR WHAT YOU GOT | William DeVaughn |
| 19 | TELL ME SOMETHING GOOD | Rufus & Chaka Khan |
| 20 | LIVIN' FOR YOU | Al Green |

# TOP SOUL SINGLES OF THE YEAR – 1975

| | | |
|---|---|---|
| 1 | FIGHT THE POWER (Part 1) | Isley Brothers |
| 2 | FIRE | The Ohio Players |
| 3 | GET DOWN TONIGHT | K C & The Sunshine Band |
| 4 | LOVE WON'T LET ME WAIT | Major Harris |
| 5 | I BELONG TO YOU | Love Unlimited |
| 6 | LOOK AT ME | Moments |
| 7 | THE HUSTLE | Van McCoy & The Soul City Symphony |
| 8 | ROCKIN' CHAIR | Gwen McCrae |
| 9 | PICK UP THE PIECES | Average White Band |
| 10 | SHINING STAR | Earth, Wind, & Fire |
| 11 | YOUR LOVE | Graham Central Station |
| 12 | GET DOWN, GET DOWN | Joe Simon |
| 13 | BABY THAT'S BACK AT 'CHA | Smokey Robinson |
| 14 | L-O-V-E | Al Green |
| 15 | THIS WILL BE | Natalie Cole |
| 16 | GIVE THE PEOPLE WHAT THEY WANT | O'Jays |
| 17 | BOOGIE ON REGGAE WOMAN | Stevie Wonder |
| 18 | I FEEL A SONG | Gladys Knight & The Pips |
| 19 | YOU'RE THE FIRST, THE LAST, MY EVERYTHING | Barry White |
| 20 | SOONER OR LATER | The Impressions |

# TOP SOUL SINGLES OF THE YEAR – 1976

| | | |
|---|---|---|
| 1 | DISCO LADY | Johnnie Taylor |
| 2 | SOMETHING HE CAN FEEL | Aretha Franklin |
| 3 | KISS AND SAY GOODBYE | The Manhattans |
| 4 | SHAKE YOUR BOOTY | K C & The Sunshine Band |
| 5 | YOU'LL NEVER FIND ANOTHER LOVE LIKE MINE | Lou Rawls |
| 6 | GETAWAY | Earth, Wind, & Fire |
| 7 | MISTY BLUE | Dorothy Moore |
| 8 | SING A SONG | Earth, Wind, & Fire |
| 9 | SWEET THING | Rufus & Chaka Khan |
| 10 | BOOGIE FEVER | Sylvers |
| 11 | WAKE UP EVERYBODY (Part 1) | Harold Melvin & The Bluenotes |
| 12 | PLAY THAT FUNKY MUSIC | Wild Cherry |
| 13 | YOUNG HEARTS RUN FREE | Candi Staton |
| 14 | TURNING POINT | Tyrone Davis |
| 15 | SOPHISTICATED LADY | Natalie Cole |
| 16 | HEAVEN MUST BE MISSING AN ANGEL (Part l) | Tavares |
| 17 | WHO'D SHE COO | The Ohio Players |
| 18 | I LOVE MUSIC (Part l) | O'Jays |
| 19 | GET UP OFFA' THAT THING | James Brown |
| 20 | LIVIN' FOR THE WEEKEND | O'Jays |

# TOP SOUL SINGLES OF THE YEAR – 1977

| | | |
|---|---|---|
| 1 | FLOAT ON | The Floaters |
| 2 | I'VE GOT LOVE ON MY MIND | Natalie Cole |
| 3 | GOT TO GIVE IT UP | Marvin Gaye |
| 4 | I WISH | Stevie Wonder |
| 5 | BEST OF MY LOVE | The Emotions |
| 6 | DAZZ | Brick |
| 7 | TRYING TO LOVE TWO | William Bell |
| 8 | IT'S ECSTASY WHEN YOU LAY DOWN NEXT TO ME | Barry White |
| 9 | STRAWBERRY LETTER 23 | Brothers Johnson |
| 10 | SLIDE | Slave |
| 11 | GOOD THING MAN | Frank Lucas |
| 12 | DON'T LEAVE ME THIS WAY | Thelma Houston |
| 13 | CAR WASH | Rose Royce |
| 14 | EASY | The Commodores |
| 15 | SUNSHINE | Enchantment |
| 16 | FREE | Deniece Williams |
| 17 | AIN'T GONNA' BUMP NO MORE | Joe Tex |
| 18 | GLORIA | Enchantment |
| 19 | I BELIEVE YOU | Dorothy Moore |
| 20 | SOMETIMES | Facts Of Life |

# TOP SOUL SINGLES OF THE YEAR – 1978

| | | |
|---|---|---|
| 1 | SERPENTINE FIRE | Earth, Wind & Fire |
| 2 | USE TO BE MY GIRL | O'Jays |
| 3 | TOO MUCH, TOO LITTLE, TOO LATE | Johnny Mathis & Deniece Williams |
| 4 | FLASHLIGHT | Parliament |
| 5 | ONE NATION UNDER A GROOVE | Funkadelic |
| 6 | OUR LOVE | Natalie Cole |
| 7 | BOOGIE OOGIE OOGIE | A Taste of Honey |
| 8 | YOU AND I | Rick James |
| 9 | CLOSE THE DOOR | Teddy Pendergrass |
| 10 | FFUN | Con Funk Shun |
| 11 | THE CLOSER I GET TO YOU | Robert Flack & Donny Hathaway |
| 12 | GET OFF | Foxy |
| 13 | TAKE ME TO THE NEXT PHASE | Isley Brothers |
| 14 | WHICH WAY IS UP | Stargard |
| 15 | THREE TIMES A LADY | The Commodores |
| 16 | STUFF LIKE THAT | Quincy Jones |
| 17 | BOOTZILLA | Bootsy's Rubber Band |
| 18 | IT'S YOU THAT I NEED | Enchantment |
| 19 | DANCE WITH ME | Peter Brown |
| 20 | HOLDING ON | LTD |

# TOP SOUL SINGLES OF THE YEAR – 1979

| | | |
|---|---|---|
| 1 | GOOD TIMES | Chic |
| 2 | RING MY BELL | Anita Ward |
| 3 | DON'T STOP 'TIL YOU GET ENOUGH | Michael Jackson |
| 4 | BUSTIN' LOOSE | Chuck Brown & The Soul Searchers |
| 5 | LE FREAK | Chic |
| 6 | AQUA BOOGIE | Parliament |
| 7 | REUNITED | Peaches & Herb |
| 8 | I GOT MY MIND MADE UP | Instant Funk |
| 9 | I'M EVERY WOMAN | Chaka Khan |
| 10 | DISCO NIGHTS | GQ |
| 11 | ONE NATION UNDER A GROOVE | Funkadelic |
| 12 | SHAKE YOUR BODY | The Jacksons |
| 13 | AIN'T NO STOPPIN' US NOW | McFadden & Whitehead |
| 14 | TURN OFF THE LIGHTS | Teddy Pendergrass |
| 15 | GOT TO BE REAL | Cheryl Lynn |
| 16 | BAD GIRLS | Donna Summer |
| 17 | WHAT 'CHA GONNA' DO WITH MY LOVIN' | Stephanie Mills |
| 18 | WHY LEAVE US ALONE | Five Special |
| 19 | DO YOU WANNA' GO PARTY | K C & The Sunshine Band |
| 20 | YOU'RE GONNA MAKE ME LOVE SOMEBODY ELSE | The Jones Girls |

# TOP SOUL SINGLES OF THE YEAR – 1980

| | | |
|---|---|---|
| 1 | LET'S GET SERIOUS | Jermaine Jackson |
| 2 | ROCK WITH YOU | Michael Jackson |
| 3 | TAKE YOUR TIME | The SOS Band |
| 4 | THE SECOND TIME AROUND | Shalamar |
| 5 | AND THE BEAT GOES ON | The Whispers |
| 6 | ONE IN A MILLION YOU | Larry Graham |
| 7 | DO YOU LOVE WHAT YOU FEEL | Rufus & Chaka Khan |
| 8 | DON'T SAY GOODNIGHT | Isley Brothers |
| 9 | I WANNA' BE YOUR LOVER | Prince |
| 10 | LADIES NIGHT | Kool & the Gang |
| 11 | CRUISIN' | Smokey Robinson |
| 12 | SPECIAL LADY | Ray, Goodman, & Brown |
| 13 | STOMP | The Brothers Johnson |
| 14 | SHINING STAR | The Manhattans |
| 15 | FUNKYTOWN | Lipps, Inc |
| 16 | KNEE DEEP | Funkadelic |
| 17 | GIVE ME THE NIGHT | George Benson |
| 18 | SWEET SENSATION | Stephanie Mills |
| 19 | UPSIDE DOWN | Diana Ross |
| 20 | ALL NIGHT THING | The Invisible Man's Band |

# Artists Inducted into
# The Rock and Roll Hall of Fame

# 1986 – 2009

**Note:** The Rock and Roll Hall of Fame inducted its first group of musicians on January 23, 1986.

# Artists Inducted into
# The Rock and Roll Hall of Fame

## 2009
Jeff Beck
Little Anthony & the Imperials
Metallica
Run-D.M.C.
Bobby Womack
Wanda Jackson
Bill Black
DJ Fontana
Spooner Oldham

## 2008
John Mellencamp
Leonard Cohen
Madonna
The Dave Clark Five
The Ventures

## 2007
Grandmaster Flash and the Furious Five
Patti Smith
R.E.M.
The Ronettes
Van Halen

## 2006

Black Sabbath
Blondie
Lynyrd Skynyrd
Miles Davis
Sex Pistols

## 2005

Buddy Guy
Percy Sledge
The O'Jays
The Pretenders
U2

## 2004

Bob Seger
George Harrison
Jackson Browne
Prince
The Dells
Traffic
ZZ Top

## 2003

AC/DC
Elvis Costello & the Attractions
Righteous Brothers
The Clash
The Police

## 2002

Brenda Lee
Gene Pitney
Isaac Hayes
Ramones
Talking Heads
Tom Petty and the Heartbreakers

## 2001

Aerosmith
Michael Jackson
Paul Simon
Queen
Ritchie Valens
Solomon Burke
Steely Dan
The Flamingos

## 2000

Bonnie Raitt
Earth, Wind & Fire
Eric Clapton
James Taylor
Lovin' Spoonful
The Moonglows

# 1999

Billy Joel
Bruce Springsteen
Curtis Mayfield
Del Shannon
Dusty Springfield
Paul McCartney
The Staple Singers

# 1998

Fleetwood Mac
Gene Vincent
Lloyd Price
Santana
The Eagles
The Mamas and the Papas

# 1997

Buffalo Springfield
Crosby Stills and Nash
Joni Mitchell
Parliament-Funkadelic
The (Young) Rascals
The Bee Gees
The Jackson 5

# 1996

David Bowie
Gladys Knight and the Pips
Jefferson Airplane
Little Willie John
Pink Floyd
The Shirelles
The Velvet Underground

# 1995

Al Green
Frank Zappa
Janis Joplin
Led Zeppelin
Martha and the Vandellas
Neil Young
The Allman Brothers Band

# 1994

Bob Marley
Duane Eddy
Elton John
John Lennon
Rod Stewart
The Animals
The Band
The Grateful Dead

## 1993

Cream
Creedence Clearwater Revival
Etta James
Frankie Lymon and the Teenagers
Ruth Brown
Sly and the Family Stone
The Doors
Van Morrison

## 1992

Bobby "Blue" Bland
Booker T. and the M.G.'s
Johnny Cash
Sam and Dave
The Isley Brothers
The Jimi Hendrix Experience
The Yardbirds

## 1991

Ike and Tina Turner
Jimmy Reed
John Lee Hooker
LaVern Baker
The Byrds
The Impressions
Wilson Pickett

# 1990

Bobby Darin
Hank Ballard
Simon and Garfunkel
The Four Seasons
The Four Tops
The Kinks
The Platters
The Who


# 1989

Dion
Otis Redding
Stevie Wonder
The Rolling Stones
The Temptations


# 1988

Bob Dylan
The Beach Boys
The Beatles
The Drifters
The Supremes

# 1987

Aretha Franklin
B.B. King
Big Joe Turner
Bill Haley
Bo Diddley
Carl Perkins
Clyde McPhatter
Eddie Cochran
Jackie Wilson
Marvin Gaye
Muddy Waters
Ricky Nelson
Roy Orbison
Smokey Robinson
The Coasters

# 1986

Buddy Holly
Chuck Berry
Elvis Presley
Fats Domino
James Brown
Jerry Lee Lewis
Little Richard
Ray Charles
Sam Cooke
The Everley Brothers

# Resources

# Resources

**Best websites to find music lyrics**
I have listed these sites that contain the most lyrics. While this is not intended to be a comprehensive list of websites that provide lyrics, many websites I found contain annoying pop-ups and offers that are oftentimes difficult to escape. The following sites contain little advertising and allows you to navigate the site free of the maze of advertising and pop-ups.

- http://www.lyricsfreak.com
- http://www.absolutelyrics.com
- http://www.songfacts.com
- http://www.lyrics.com


**Best websites to find the album, all tracts on the album and the year it was released together with the lyrics.**

- http://www.absolutelyrics.com
- http://www.gracenote.com


**Best websites to find general information on an artist; the current Top 100 songs; and lists of the best rock artists, musicians, albums, concerts, etc.**

- http://www.wikipedia.org

  *The easiest, most comprehensive resource for finding information on an artist or group to include detailed history as well as a chronological list of all albums and singles released by the artist.*

- http://www.billboard.com

  *The authoritative site that gives you the latest Top 100 records and albums; however, a subscription is required to get access to historical information.*

- http://www.pollstar.com

  *The authoritative source for concerts both current and historical summaries of top concerts by year, broken down by various categories such as top grossing concerts, highest attendances, number of sold out concerts, etc.*

- http://digitaldreamdoor.nutsie.com

  *A great website to find lists of the all-time greatest rock guitarists, drummers, albums, songs, etc.*

- http://www.answers.com

  *This website is good to find general information on artists and links to other relevant websites but it is not as comprehensive as Wikipedia.org*

## Best websites to download music
- http://www.amazon.com
- http://www.apple.com/itunes

## Rock and Roll Hall of Fame Website
- http://www.rockhall.com

# Index

Breinigsville, PA USA
22 February 2010
232990BV00003B/37/P